The Faith of Jesus

The Jesus of History
and the
Stages of Faith

by

Richard W. Kropf

Wipf and Stock Publishers
Eugene, Oregon

Wipf and Stock Publishers
199 West Eighth Avenue, Suite 3
Eugene, Oregon 97401

The Faith of Jesus: The Jesus of History and the Stages of Faith
By Kropf, Richard W. 1932-
Copyright© April 2005 by Kropf, Richard W.
ISBN: 978-1-4982-4748-1
Publication date: January, 2006

Contents

Contents

Foreword

Let us not lose sight of Jesus, who leads us in our
faith and brings it to perfection...   (Hebrews 12:2a)

Did Jesus have faith? If we can believe the words from the Letter to the Hebrews just quoted, there seems no question about it. Yet how few Christians (and I include translators of scripture among them) have been able to take this testimony at its worth. Instead we have hedged around the subject, more often than not to the detriment of our own faith. A typical example is fixed in my own memory.

Some years ago, an elderly aunt of mine who was broken in health and quite out of her senses had to be confined to a convalescent home. I attempted to console her daughter who was very upset and angry with God for allowing her mother to suffer so. When I tried to point out to her that her mother really didn't seem to realize where she was, or even who we were, and that she (my cousin) was in fact suffering more than her mother, she couldn't accept these remarks. So then I added, "But see what God allowed his own son to suffer on the cross! What did Jesus do to deserve that?" To that she replied, "Oh but that's different, after all, he [Jesus] was God!"

Her response has been on my mind ever since. Did the divinity of Christ somehow diminish his sufferings? Or were his pains purely a physical ordeal that he had to go through, even while remaining secure in the certain knowledge that in a few hours his agony would be all over and that in a few days he would rise triumphantly from the dead?

If so, then I began to wonder just what relevance Jesus' life and death really had to ours? Was it some kind of charade meant simply to reassure us with the certainty of another world beyond, and if so, why would it be necessary for God to actually become a human to give us this reassurance? Would not a prophet displaying a few miracles, perhaps raising a few more people from the dead, be enough? Or how about just someone returning from that other world now and then to remind us that there is another life beyond? All or any of these alternatives would seem good enough for me.

1

What about the millions upon millions of people in the world who find the Christian belief that Jesus was (and is) in fact God in human form to be a claim that is simply incomprehensible, if not blasphemous as well? Are they not, at least in some sense, correct? How can we make any sense out of the assertion that he is both fully God as well as fully man? We may feel put out by such attempts to stress the humanity of Jesus, as for example, Martin Scorcese's infamous film based on the Kazantzakis novel, *The Last Temptation of Christ*. Many deemed it heretical, even if blasphemy was not intended. But does not our tendency as Christians to hedge around and avoid the full implications of his humanity, if not blasphemous, amount to heresy as well?

It is questions like these, and experiences like that with my cousin —who after that incident, lost two of her four children in tragic circumstances and who had to face a prolonged illness before her own death—that have convinced me that for far too many Christians the belief in the true humanity of Jesus has been all but eclipsed by belief in his divinity. And with that eclipse has come the diminishment of our ability to appreciate and identify fully with what God has accomplished for us in Christ, including leading us personally in the path of faith.

If this overall approach still bothers some readers, I would suggest that perhaps they should read the final chapter (subtitled "A Christological Postscript") first to decide whether it can be squared with Christian faith. Beyond that, I can only plead again the case of so many others who, like my cousin, have found little or no consolation in a divine Christ who dominates over humanity rather than suffers with us. It is to those like her, and perhaps even more, to those who struggle to help those in similar situations, that this book, which grew out of workshops and retreats based on my earlier book, *Faith: Security and Risk*, is dedicated.

Richard W. Kropf
Montmorency County
Michigan
December, 2005

Introduction

The Jesus of History and the Stages of Faith

It has been estimated that in recent decades more books have been written and published about Jesus Christ than in the entire past history of Christianity. Despite the warning of modern scholars about those who peer narcissistically into their own prejudices to produce a Jesus to their own liking, it seems that many, including some of the scholars themselves, have been engaged in writing his or her own version of the gospel story, each one blending the facts, to the extent that we know them, to come up with an interpretation to suit personal purposes and insights. This book is probably no different. It is, very simply, my own attempt at a "Life of Christ".

I have already stated my purpose in the *Foreword*: it is to make the figure of Jesus more credible as a real historical human being who was, at the same time, preeminently, a person of faith.

The Historical Question

Leaving aside the bizarre opinion of those who deny that Jesus of Nazareth ever lived, no one who sets his or her mind to the task of writing anything on this subject can afford paying some attention to the work of all those scholars, who beginning early in the last century or even a little before, have struggled, in the so-called "Quest for the Historical Jesus" as distinguished from the "Christ of Faith". Despite the impression that this quest has been motivated by an attempt to tear down belief in Jesus Christ—as may have been the case in a few instances—the vast majority of these scholars has been most of all moved by a desire to make the figure of Christ more believable and less remote to human experience. Their efforts, of course, launched that whole movement of modern biblical "criticism" or scholarship, a quest that is far from over even today. Nor do I wish to be accused of ignoring this important quest. I will, for example, make liberal use of the almost universally accepted (even by the Vatican's official Biblical Commission) distinction between the three layers or levels of tradition as found in the sources, that is, in the gospels themselves.

3

The first layer is the actual record of the sayings and at least some of the deeds of Jesus. That there happens to be a wide range of opinions as to what actually belongs to this memory of the historical Jesus does not change the fact that there was such a person and that he made a profound impression on those whom heard and witnessed him. Nor can there be little doubt that this impression also set the stage for his execution.

The second layer of this tradition, however, has a scope that goes beyond what Jesus may have actually said and done. This layer represents the development of the *kerygma* or "gospel" (good news) message that proclaims the meaning of the life and death of Jesus for those who choose to follow him—the most outstanding claim of which is that the ignominious death of Jesus as a supposed criminal was but the prelude to his resurrection from the dead, a saving event that will forever change the course of history and the fate of the human race.

Finally, beyond the fundamental message or meaning attached to his life by those who believed in him, there was created a third, or primarily theological layer of exposition. It is this third level that gives each of the four traditionally accepted gospels its own distinctive outlook, each of which seems to have been addressed to meet a particular need—for example, Luke's particular attempt to present a Jesus who is more comprehensible to the non-Jewish world.

Although I will attempt to make ample use of these distinctions when they fit my purpose, I must point out some problems introduced by them as well.

The first problem is the most potentially damaging to any project like mine. It is simply that, in the opinion of many of the foremost scholars today, any attempt to construct a "life of Jesus", in the manner of a biography, including a more or less agreed upon calendar of events making up his public life, is doomed from the start. It has been long recognized that the order of particular events as presented in the Gospel According to John does not adhere closely to that presented by the other three gospels (the "synoptics") and that those of Matthew and Luke borrowed more or less loosely from the story line found in Mark. In other words, the more or less detailed sequence of events presented by the gospels is pretty much a third level tradition. The most primitive or primary level of tradition, the only part that is undoubtedly historical in the modern sense (excluding his execution and probably his baptism) are the scattered recollections of his sayings and the reports of some of the astounding deeds that were said to have often accompanied them. So, obviously, we have a problem here!

Nevertheless, I will foolishly forge forward on what may seem to at first be merely a hunch. However, I think it is a lot more than merely that. It is based on what seems to me to be the most obviously historical fact of all—that Jesus of Nazareth was a living person who, no matter how famous or controversial he may have become, was nevertheless a human being much as the rest of us. Although the fundamental conditions of human living may have changed greatly since that time, human nature itself has not changed all that much. Humans are still conceived, born, and to a large extent develop physically and psychologically, much as they always have and probably always will. Add to this the fact that even the story, in its basic outlines, (whether it be a creation of Mark or anyone else, or actually a remembrance of the sequence of events as they really happened) logically fits, almost to a "T" as they say, what was to prove to be its recorded outcome—not just by the gospel writers but by a few non-Christian historians of that era. In fact, some scholars believe that even the story of the end of John the Baptist was retold to resemble that of Jesus. All this seems to me to be of great significance. Ask any playwright, for example, to tell a story of a would-be religious reformer who attracts a large following and ends up being executed by the authorities who want things to remain as they are, and you are bound to get a plot not unlike that presented by the gospels. Such an outcome is almost, as they used to say, "written in the stars." So I have no problem in following the story line presented by the synoptic gospels, and even using a bit of John's own story line, as representing what in all probability actually took place.

Yet there is a further problem. For even as I have tried to utilize the results of this historical quest, I have found myself forced, by the logic of the insights that I wish to bring to this study, to emphasize some aspects of the gospel story that modern biblical scholarship tends to discount as especially questionable. Among these is the story of the finding of the child Jesus in the temple, the temptations in the desert, his Transfiguration and even (in my treatment of the Resurrection faith) his so-called "Descent into Hell", which although this latter is not mentioned in the gospels, is an old scripture-based theme. Any mention of these, particularly of the latter, is bound to conjure up theories of religious myth designed to assure the reader that these events are not to be taken literally. But as Joseph Campbell has taught us, are they not to be taken seriously nonetheless? If myth is not to be understood as a vehicle of existential truth (as kind of truth that as one author put it, never "happened" but nevertheless "is") then religious belief is indeed in a bad way.

However, the reason I choose to single out these stories is not primarily based on any enlightened view of the meaning of myth or on the rejection of historical criticism. Instead, most of all, it has to do with the realm of psychology in general, and more specifically developmental psychology and with what has become recently recognized and closely studied in terms of the phenomenon known as the "stages of faith".

Faith Stages

No doubt that any mention of the word "psychology" in this context will cause all the warning flags to go up. If there is any kind of speculation that upsets the typical academic biblical scholar more than conjectures of what may or may have not been the psychological state of Jesus at any given time, I don't know what else it might be. Descriptions of Jesus as having rejoiced, been saddened, to have wept, or that he groaned, or that he sometimes got outright angry, seem to bother no one just as long as people like me don't suggest what the reasons might conceivably have been for these expressions of emotion. No doubt, most of these depictions belong to the third level or story line of the tradition, but again, I would suggest that a logical basis for such expressions (whether they took place at the occasions as described in the gospels or not) would be in the structure of the human psyche itself—something that again I presume that Jesus shared with the rest of us. In fact, the only logical reason I can really find for denying ourselves some plausibly valid insights into the mental and psychological processes that probably did in fact take place in Jesus' mind would be the denial that he had a mind that worked in ways similar to ours. But such an opinion, despite its repeated occurrence down through history (similar to the incident described in the *Foreword*), was long ago condemned as being heretical.

It is for this reason that I will make no further apologies for treating the possibility of something like Luke's story of the finding of the child Jesus in the Temple as being highly plausible, even if not historically verifiable, or the visionary experience on Mt. Tabor—no matter how confounding to modern prejudices—as being, very possibly, *the* historical turning point of Jesus' own decision to carry out what he understood to be his mission, cost what it might. The fact that such incidents may have been added to the story by the evangelists as so-called *theologumena* or "God-talk" does not bother me all that much. If anyone knows anything about the lives of mystics, prophets, and even some philosophers, such psychic events are all more real, at least in terms of what motivated their outlook and behavior, than most other things in the story of their lives.

Thus, unlike most of the scholarly "questers" after the historical Jesus, I have not attempted to get aside these later levels of tradition to concentrate on the actual words and deeds of Jesus alone. Instead, I have tried to use the results of their quest to clear the deck, as it were, to make room for a new approach, a new theological "slant"—even a new "third level" interpretation if you will—where the second level message or *kerygma* supplies the guidelines as to where my own quest is taking me.

Just what is this insight or approach? Again, as I hope the title of this book, as well as the personal story I recounted in my *Foreword*, tried to make clear, it is an attempt to apply a faith stage analysis to the story of Jesus in hopes that his life can be more effectively a model for ours.

The research that led to such a concept as faith stages originally had nothing to do with religion or belief. It has its roots in the developmental theories of psychiatrist Erik Erikson and especially in the pioneering work of the Swiss educational psychologist Jean Piaget, who years back did extensive studies on the cognitive stages of growth in the reasoning processes of young boys. There were no big surprises, except the suspicion that many adults continue to reason in similar ways, confirming what later feminist critics are right to point out, even if in a different context, that "boys will be boys".

Piaget's findings were then used for a similar series of studies, but this time focused particularly on moral reasoning, by the American psychologist Lawrence Kohlberg. In this case, the results were rather upsetting, especially when correlated to adult methods of moral reasoning. It seems that few of the subjects progressed much farther than the kind of immediate group and peer loyalty, with its notion of "fairness" as the norm of justice, that is usually reached in the latter stages of childhood or early adolescence. Further studies have shown that most adults, unless effectively challenged to go beyond that stage of moral reasoning, rarely do so.

Now I think that this is highly significant when it comes to understanding the impact of Jesus on his own society—unless we are to suppose that in that time and place people were already generally advanced beyond what seems the norm now. In some aspects perhaps they were, but across-the-board, I doubt it very much. Clearly Jesus was preaching on a new stage of moral development, one that while it attracted large numbers of the general population, at the same time caused the authorities to become alarmed. Any rabble-rouser could have of course, caused such an effect. But it is clear that the effect recorded by the gospels, particularly by those passages that make up The Sermon on the Mount, was a call to a new level of religious and moral consciousness.

Which leads up more specifically to the stages of faith. Following Kohlberg's lead, theologian James W. Fowler developed further set of tests, one that focused on the understandings and attitude generally associated with faith or religious beliefs, and found a much similar result. While having moved beyond the earliest stages of faith, the majority of adults showed signs of not having advanced in their understanding of their religious beliefs in any way that much differed from those reached in their early teens. Thus most adults seem to be comfortable with what can be called an entirely *"conventional"* stage of faith, one which identifies one's religious faith with ones family, nationality, or ethnic group. This is not to imply that this allegiance is insincere. But it is often confused with other things that have nothing to do with religion.

On the other hand, in Fowler's study there was a significant minority who showed considerable personal commitment that is quite independent of the above factors, even though it may still coincide with them. Here we have the occurrence of what I call a truly *"personal"* faith, one that has to be taken seriously as a commitment made by an individual quite conscious of what is at stake. In other words, at the heart of such personal faith is a kind of *conversion* experience, at least in the sense of a deliberate owning up to what has been up to that time largely taken for granted. Some, no doubt in a more emotional sense, call this a "born-again" experience. Others, taking a more intellectual approach, may simply see it as taking ones own religion seriously.

However, beyond that stage, there is one that Fowler has termed "paradoxical-consolidative" but which I have called *"conjunctive"*. It is characterized perhaps by what might be thought of as a broader or more philosophical point of view, one in which there is a certain openness towards others' points of view or towards persons that their own society tended to reject. It seems to be an attitude that is more concerned about people's well-being than about their religious affiliation, about doing good things rather than about identity or loyalty to any particular group. Here the conflict between Jesus and the Pharisees, at least as the latter are depicted in the gospels—which is to say hardly in a complimentary way—if not entirely accurate, nevertheless highlights the difference. Both are sincerely committed to what they believe. The charge of "hypocrite" may not be a very accurate translation here, as at least some of these fellows apparently really did believe you could lose your soul by failing to wash your dishes. Jesus just believed there were much more important issues at stake and more important standards by which one would be judged than whether one was an observant Jew or not.

Finally, Fowler's analysis holds up a higher stage yet, one which he calls "universalizing" but which I call *"unitive"*. Unfortunately it is so rare we are given to calling such people "saints", even though a lot of the folk given this title down through history had some glaring faults nonetheless. Some were great mystics, others were martyrs, some neither, but in general, they seem to be people who try, as much as they can, to live in constant awareness of God and in constant obedience to God's will as they understand it. Not all of them, by a long shot, have been Christians. Yet how much they still remind us of Jesus!

This brings up the final challenge that has to be considered before we examine his faith and his life. Why is it that so few people succeed in emulating his example—or even try to? The answer to this question forms what might be called the base note or background theme of this book. It has to do with the very nature of faith.

The Risk of Faith

It should be understood, despite the widespread confusion between the two words, that "faith" is *not* the same as "belief". People believe all sorts of things, many of them not having the slightest thing to do with faith in any theological sense of the word. Faith in the biblical meaning of the Hebrew word *emunah,* and especially in the gospel meaning of the Greek word *pistis*, has primarily to do with *trust*. No doubt this trust is founded on certain beliefs, but without the *commitment* that trust demands, there can be no real faith.

Nor does the commitment of faith mean the same as "confidence" despite the inclusion of the Latin word for faith (*fides*) in that much-desired attitude towards life. Confidence, like security, is but a by-product of a life of faith, and as a by-product, much like happiness or fulfillment, can never successfully become an end or goal in itself. (See especially the discussion of Viktor Frankl's psycho-dynamics in chapters 1 and 2 of my earlier book on the subject.) God will not be used as a self-enhancement program or as a security blanket. Real faith is not refuge from life. It involves just the opposite. Hence it must be made clear that real faith involves *risk,* and that risk is really, when one comes down to it, a matter of defining the whole meaning of our life in terms of what we believe to be our responsibility to God and to the world.

Thus the risk involved in living the life of faith, a risk multiplied by the fact that this belief cannot be certain knowledge. As St. Paul put it, "We walk by faith and not by sight" (2 Corinthians 5:7). No one, when making a commitment, knows exactly what the outcome might be. Otherwise, a commitment would not be necessary. The security of knowing that all will turn out well is nice to have, but if we were absolutely certain, we would have no more need for faith.

All this suggests that the failure to grow in faith, the inability to risk the consolation afforded by ones present stage of faith, is itself the greatest obstacle to any further growth. How else explain the unspeakable crimes committed down through history in the name of religion or the religious intolerance that even today pits one "true believer" against another? Do such attitudes manifest any real trust in God? By any stretch of the imagination can this be said to be what Jesus taught? If Jesus steadfastly refused either to be intimidated by his opponents, or to strike back at them or in any way to coerce them, but instead chose to suffer persecution in resolute dedication to his mission as he saw it, it was because *love,* and the *faith* and *hope* that flowed from it, were the primary motive forces of his life.

This is why I propose Jesus as a model for us. In an age of disbelief—or, I should say rather in an age that is ready to believe anything, providing it produces good feeling—I'd say that it is Jesus who most of all presents to us an example of genuine and radical faith. And it was without doubt a faith that grew in intensity the more it was challenged by the risk-taking demanded by his mission to the world. Thus it is that the faith *of* Jesus—and by this I mean the faith that Jesus himself had in the God whom he called his "Father"—must be the great exemplar for our own faith. Otherwise, can we really claim to be his followers in the footsteps of his "race" to do the Father's will?

This is also why I have put so much weight in the passage found in the twelfth chapter of the Epistle to the Hebrews—not just because it is the one place in scripture that refers so directly to Jesus as our "leader in faith", despite the long history of mistranslation to avoid facing the full force of that statement (see the appendix at the end of this book for details about the doctoring of Hebrews 12:1b-2a). It is this epistle, which is absolutely unstinting of its avowal and praise of Jesus as the "Son of God" (see especially Hebrews 1:2-3), that repeatedly calls Christians to follow him in the marathon-like race by which he (and eventually we) reach our reward.

There are, I realize, many people, not all of them Bible translators or theologians, for whom my approach raises difficulties. After all, is not Jesus divine? Would he have not, as Son of God, already known all that he needed to know as a man? How could Jesus be said to have had "faith"? In this way, our belief in Christ's divinity has all too often acted like a set of blinders that have prevented us from seeing clearly what is all too obvious to those who read the scriptures without prejudice—that Jesus had his own set of convictions, and that even some of these, at least in part, may have been incomplete or subject to revision as time went on.

No doubt some will say that in suggesting this, I have fixed my own set of blinders to establish my own prejudice and an agenda to go with it—that of trying to humanize Christ and make him just like one of us. If by "just" it is implied that he was simply the same as us in every way, then no, I would deny this charge. I believe that "no man has spoken as this man" (John 7:46), nor has any mere man lived as this one. But still, I am trying to see Jesus in his full humanity. I don't think I can try to fool the reader about that. Here I believe that I stand in full solidarity with those early Church theologians who made it their maxim, in the face of those who would water down Jesus' humanity to leave more room for his divinity, that "What wasn't assumed wasn't redeemed." Accordingly, I would argue that if Jesus truly existed as a living, breathing, human being, he had to live to some extent, as the "just man" on "faith alone" (see Romans 4:3; James 2:23).

I realize that it may be that this image of Jesus who runs the race of faith before us and leads us to its completion has to be reconciled with that of the glorified Son of God who is "the radiant light of God's glory and the perfect copy of his nature" (Hebrews 1:3). I think that simply making both assertions, even if that is what the Epistle to the Hebrews does, is not enough. Human understanding, being limited, tends to latch onto one side or another of what seems to be a contradiction in terms. In addition, while certain ancient world-views or modes of thinking may have provided what seemed to be, in past ages, something like a solution to this problem, no matter how precarious or unsatisfactory, more contemporary understandings—for example of human nature understood in an evolutionary context—may provide us with a fresh start to addressing such difficulties, even though the language employed in such effort may strike traditionalists as quite unorthodox. For this reason, I have added a final chapter on "Faith in Christ", a kind of "Christological Postscript", in which I have attempted to sketch my approach to keeping this balance and to which readers are invited to turn at any time if they harbor suspicions that I have already lost it. But they must understand that this book is first of all concerned with contemplating the faith *of* Jesus, while the task of achieving a metaphysical understanding of our faith *in* the Christ as both God and man is quite another thing. It would have be the task of another book, one that would turn out to be much longer than this attempt.

Chapter 1

Beginnings

In this chapter we will consider the first four stages of faith, those that generally cover the years from birth to young adulthood, even as they might be applied to what little we know of the background and early years of Jesus.

In fact, we know very little for sure. In terms of the three levels of tradition in the Gospels, it is hard to say that the infancy narratives of Matthew and Luke contain anything other than third level, theological elaboration, using material that appears to be legendary in origin. Clearly these accounts do not claim to record the actual words and deeds of Jesus, at least not in the way considered essential for the kind of apostolic witness laid down in Acts 1:15-26. Nor, for that matter, do the stories even agree, except on a few basic points: first, that Jesus was conceived by the power of the Holy Spirit in the womb of a woman called Mary who was espoused to, but apparently was not yet living with, a man named Joseph; second, that the child was born in Bethlehem of Judea: and third, that later they made their way back to their residence in Nazareth in the Northern province of Galilee. Other than these basic assertions, that's really all that they agree on. (See Raymond E. Brown, 1977.)

But are even these three areas of agreement really historical facts? Obviously Jesus had to have been born. But do we really know for sure exactly where and when? Luke tries to link Jesus' birth to an imperial census taken while a certain Quirinius was governor of Syria (6-7 AD), but that is surely much too late. All other calculations point to a more likely date for Jesus' birth as being between 6-4 BCE. Nor is there any verifiable historical evidence, other than the rather early veneration of the cave-grotto at Bethlehem, of that town, approximately five miles south of Jerusalem, really having been the place of his birth. As far as history knows him, our Jesus was *Yeshua bar Yosef,* the carpenter from Nazareth in Galilee, about seventy-five miles north of Jerusalem.

So, exactly what are the infancy narratives of Matthew and Luke really meant to tell us? Or even to what extent are they part of the *kerygma* or "proclamation" of the Gospel or "Good News" as preached by the Apostles—the second level or category of gospel material as recognized by contemporary scholars?

Here we have a problem, because although some of this background material made it into the official Christian creeds ("conceived by the Holy Spirit, born of the Virgin Mary", etc.) it is quite obvious that the earliest apostolic message did not include such details of Jesus' origin or birth, other than, much as Paul says, that he "was a descendent of the family of David" (Romans 1:3)—a claim that some would consider questionable—and "born of a woman, born a subject of the law" (Galatians 4:4).

Add to this the lack of any infancy narrative in John's Gospel—unless we persist in trying to see the words about those "who were born not of natural generation nor by human choice nor by man's decision" in the prologue (John 1:13) as being an allusion to this approach—we can only conclude that much like Mark's gospel, not only does the central message of Christianity as preached by the Apostles really begin with Jesus' baptism at the Jordan, but so does any claim of the gospels to be a historical record of worth.

But this is not to say that on the *theological* level these infancy narratives, like many other stories included in the gospels, do not have a profound role for us in helping us understand the essential meaning of the good news. For example, both these accounts, although again in somewhat different ways, indicate that Mary, although espoused to Joseph, was still a virgin when Jesus was conceived. Yet even here, the purpose seems to be primarily "apologetic" in the theological sense of the word. This story seems meant to convey, in a way the world might find most convincing at that time, a more basic message yet—that this man, Jesus, truly is what his name (*Yeshua* in Aramaic or *Joshua* in Hebrew) implies, that through him "God saves" and not only that, but that in him we see "the Son of God", he who is, in some mysterious way, God-with-us, *Emmanuel.*

Yet for us, I think that these stories have an additional impact, one that is quite the opposite of the more abstract theme of the descent of divine Wisdom or "Word" that we see featured in the later Pauline writings or in John. It is this same element that accounts for the popularity of the Christmas story and the infancy narratives, even among non-Christians today. It is the idea that divinity can be revealed in and through humanity, and that even God, if that is what he was, can, "grow in age and stature and grace."

So with this sparse amount of information to go on, but with confidence that he was indeed a human like ourselves, let us proceed.

The Infancy of Jesus: Instinctive Faith

Aside from the uncertainty surrounding the actual circumstances of his birth, Jesus' growing consciousness even as an infant and small child would have been presented with the same, or similar range of possibilities that all human infants face. The first contacts with parents, the routines of the household, the emerging awareness of others, relatives, family friends, neighbors, the ebb and flow of village life—all these must have had an effect, whether greater or lesser, on the attitudes and responses of this child, and in turn, shaped and formed that set of attitudes and responses that we can call "trust" or in a more specifically religious context, "faith".

Yet, to speak about "faith" in infancy presents us with much the same problem as that facing James Fowler when he first attempted to number and name the stages of faith. What does one do with a very small child? Fowler's first instinct was to speak of such faith as "undifferentiated" and assign it a zero on a scale of 0 to 6 (Fowler, 1981). Later, as the importance as the psychosomatic basis for faith in the years to come seems to have impressed Fowler in his later outlines of the stages, the first year of life becomes what amounts to Stage I, or what I call "implicit faith". (See Fowler, 1984.) This shift in emphasis is especially telling when we consider the importance of our family roots when it comes to shaping our later life.

That Jesus was a Jew among Jews should be obvious to anyone who reads the gospels even on the most superficial level. In none of these accounts, whether it be in the strident criticisms in Matthew's gospel against the Pharisees, or the almost constant conspiratorial overtones implied by John regarding the Jewish leadership, is the fact of Jesus being a Jew himself overlooked. Instead, despite it's silence regarding Jesus' circumcision and his presentation in the temple, the Gospel of Matthew goes out of its way to emphasize his Jewish identity, attempting to link him, through his presumptive father's line, to the patriarch Abraham himself and this through the family of David, Israel's most famous warrior-king.

Luke, on the other hand, the only non-Jewish evangelist, without repudiating Jesus' Jewish descent, chose to place the emphasis on his links to all humanity by symbolically tracing his ancestry clear back to Adam. Still, as we have already noted, it is only Luke that we find a clear allusion to Jesus being circumcised, which was the basic "sacrament" marking all Jewish males, and to his being offered or dedicated specially to God in a special temple ritual prescribed for all Jewish firstborn sons. It could be that Luke felt a need for his gentile readers to have more background on Jewish life and customs. But more likely, Luke saw some deep significance in the temple presentation story, even though it is a bit hard to fit in with the story of the flight into Egypt as found in Matthew's gospel. Simeon's prophecy of the child being destined for the "fall and rise of many in Israel"—whether it was really uttered or not—is meant to be an omen of sorts. Yet there is no indication of any other extraordinary occurrences in Luke's account of Jesus' infancy and early childhood. That will have to wait until later.

Infants do not grow up in a vacuum, or if they do, severe psychological damage can result. What we can see of the personality of the man Jesus leads us to conclude quite the opposite. Psychologically speaking, it is unlikely that anyone could have been such an outgoing and compassionate person as Jesus was had he been deprived of motherly nurture and love. If the common Near-Eastern pattern of mother-child relationship which is still evident today in the Arab world, where it is still often customary for male children to be nursed until age three or four—although girls are usually weaned earlier—is any indication of what was the norm back then, we must conclude that Jesus' infancy was outstandingly supportive for a future life of faith. Add to this Jesus' favored legal position as first-born son—again an advantage in most societies, even today.

Early Childhood: Intuitive Faith

If the instinctive faith of infancy consists primarily of that psychosomatic bonding of parent and child that builds up an infant's trust, the intuitive faith of early childhood sees the introduction of more clearly conscious images of that trust, images which will, in years to come, be projected as symbols of the convictions or beliefs held by faith. Clearly, it is an extremely critical stage in faith-formation. Given the wrong symbols, or distorted ones, a person's faith development can be crippled for life. Given the correct symbols, that faith, with God's grace, can blossom into a commitment that knows no bounds.

Even if we do not set aside the whole Matthean story about the flight into Egypt, and imagine that Jesus was brought back as a young child to be raised in Nazareth in the household of Mary and Joseph, we can still conclude that there was nothing extraordinary about either him or his family that attracted attention. Indeed, later in his public life it was in view of his earlier ordinariness that his relatives became quite alarmed and skeptical.

Yet future developments lead us to suppose that there must have been something going on that was much deeper. If early childhood is a time of intuitive faith, one that is learned not only from one's parents but in the image of one's parents, Jesus' extraordinary devotion to God as "Father" speaks volumes of what his early life in Nazareth must have been like, and even more of his regard for Joseph. That God be considered as a "father", so to speak, is not at all extraordinary in many of the world's religions, and certainly not out of line for Judaism with its patriarchal tradition. Yet it is hardly the favored term in the Jewish list of divine names.

By the time of Jesus, with the emphasis on the divine transcendence or "otherness", the sacred name of *Yahweh*, revealed in the scriptures and constantly invoked in the psalms, had now been all but removed from everyday or even ritual use. Jesus would never have heard the divine name pronounced in his synagogue. Instead, even when sacred letters were spelled out in the text, the reader was instructed to substitute *Adonai* or "Lord" or speak instead of *Elohim*, the generic term for God—literally "gods" (in the plural) or else use other roundabout Hebrew terms for the divinity. In the face of these taboos, we must conclude that Jesus' familiar use of *Abba* or "Father" was extraordinarily free or liberal in terms of the orthodoxy of his day. So easily did he use this word, and with such a sense of endearment, that it would be almost the equivalent of calling God "Daddy". It is apparently one of the things to which his critics objected most strongly.

How account for this? Could it have been by way of compensation? If there is anything to the old Christian tradition that is found in one of the rejected "apocryphal" gospels, a story about Joseph having been elderly at the time of Jesus' birth, then I suppose it is possible that Jesus lost Joseph's presence at some critical stage in his upbringing. But whether it was with or without Joseph's guiding presence as Jesus later grew into manhood, the sense of God as *Abba* or as a loving "Father" remained intense.

Add to this his sense of compassion, his love for nature, his love of children, his childlike sense of freedom to ignore social conventions—all these speak of an atmosphere that was trustful and warmly supportive of a childhood that was rightly summed up in Luke 2:40. "Meanwhile, the child grew to maturity. He was full of wisdom and God's favor was with him."

Late Childhood to Adolescence of Jesus: Literal Faith

Such growth does not happen all at once. Immediately after the above-quoted words, it is Luke who again gives us the most insightful story about the possible development of Jesus' faith—the story about the lost boy Jesus in the Temple, and his disconcerted parents.

According to Luke, like many pious Galileans, the parents of Jesus were in the habit of making the long journey to Jerusalem to worship at the Temple on the annual feast of the Passover. On this trip, Jesus became separated from his parents and kinfolk and was found by them, three days later, sitting among the rabbis in the Temple porch, "listening to them and asking them questions." (See Luke 2:41-50.) Those who listened to him, in turn, we are informed, "were amazed at his understanding and his answers". His parents, on the other hand, "were astonished" and seem to have hustled him home uncomprehendingly, especially after he enigmatically asked them why they bothered to look for him, especially when they should have realized he "must be about my [his] father's business". Jesus was supposed to be "about twelve years of age" at the time.

Because it has all the earmarks of a pious legend, not many modern scripture scholars have seemed to take the time to seriously investigate this story in Luke's gospel—probably because it is so patently symbolic of Jesus' future mission. But whether or not the story is an authentic recollection or even a fictionalized account of a possible occurrence, it is a story with deep significance coming at a critical point in life.

However, I am inclined to go farther and see this story as historically true precisely because the whole episode was somewhat disconcerting. Otherwise why would the evangelist admit to something so upsetting, even embarrassing, to his parents' and relatives' memory? Certainly, if the writer were indulging in pure fabrication, he would have found a more transparently edifying and consistent story to tell, one that would have stressed obedience as well as his unusualness. Instead, Luke explains this apparent lack of obedience as obedience higher call and then tells us he went home and was obedient to Joseph and Mary after all!

Even if we believe the evangelist is putting words into the young Jesus' mouth, the point of this story is that even then Jesus is pictured as being aware of his special relationship to God. Would this be possible at that age? True, the general impression of the story is one of precocity, not unlike the effect that a child prodigy in any field leaves upon those whose lives follow a more gradual pattern of development. No doubt Luke wishes to play up this aspect for all it's worth. Yet, at the same time, we should be aware that the average Jewish boy at that age was, and still is, expected to begin to undertake with all seriousness his religious observances. In some ways, this particular pilgrimage, in that year of his life, could be seen as the equivalent of the modern *Bar Mitzvah*. That Jesus is depicted as calling God his "Father" should be seen as a natural counterpart of his being now recognized as a dutiful son, that is, a Son (*Bar*) of Duty (*Mitzvah*).

But again, at this point, Luke seems to have wanted to imply a lot more. It is not simply that Jesus sees himself as a dutiful "Son of the Covenant" as it were, but, even as "Son of God". If the idea of Jews calling themselves "Sons of God"—in the sense of being God's chosen people and subservient to God's will—should not be considered exceptional at that time, so too that the young boy Jesus would have spoken of God as "my father", in much the same sense that he used the same phrase later in the gospels is hardly beyond the realm of possibility. Still, there is something special or even peculiar about the way that Jesus refers to his own relationship to God. And even if Jesus never directly, explicitly calls himself "Son of God" any place in the gospels that actually record his own words—as most scripture scholars seem to think today—still it is all of a piece. A God addressed personally as "Father" more than implies a relationship which sees oneself, even personally, and not just as part of a collective, as "Son".

Is it possible Jesus would have thought that way at age twelve? If it is the trait of childhood, even later childhood, to take another's words trustfully without qualification, then we also may have to conclude that Jesus' understanding of the God whom he had been taught to think of as *Abba* was truly as his own personal father, one to whom he owed even a higher obedience than that due his parents. If so, then this whole incident speaks of a literal faith that is without qualification, one that is "literal" in the best sense of that word.

Nevertheless, I think we have to look for another emerging quality in Jesus' faith by age twelve, a more critical one that parents today on a whole are probably more used to confronting than parents of Jesus' own time. The transition from late childhood to early adolescence is very often a time when a real religious awakening is apt to occur. It may still be far from that kind of personal conversion or commitment that takes place in later life; but still, it can represent a real threshold to a deepened religious consciousness even though it is almost of necessity bound up with all the customary and often conflicting claims of conventional religious life.

Up to this point in life, where religious observance and belief has typically been identical with one's immediate family, the widening consciousness of early adolescence generally brings about a new sense of identification with one's peers, one's culture, and, if favorably presented, with one's religious inheritance. Certainly, coming from the small provincial town of Nazareth, where Judaism had long fought a battle with alien cultural and religious currents (see Lee, 1988) the years of parental example, synagogue attendance and instruction, where he probably also learned to read and write, must have had a profound influence upon him. (See Meier, 1991, I, pp. 271-78.)

So now, even though the pilgrimage to the "high place" of Jewish piety, the temple itself, for the High Holy Days, might have an annual event for Jesus' family and friends, any such pilgrimage at this particular stage in his life could have conspired to unleash in this young man-child a new sense of identification with his religious heritage that might have overwhelmed him at the time. It could even be true that he became "lost" in his enthusiasm for the big city and ended up back in the temple as the best place to be found once he found himself separated from his kin. Who knows? Nevertheless, by the time they found him, it might have been obvious that there also was something very special about this boy who was quickly becoming a young man.

Normally, according to faith development theory, we would expect that at his age Jesus' faith up to this point would have been what is called "literal" or "literal-mythic" when it comes to the contents or intellectual convictions that constitute one's beliefs. Add to this that there would be little or no reason that even the faith of an adult, particularly in the backwater hill country of Galilee at that time, would be, at least in intellectual terms, any different from a more child-like "mythic-literal faith" in this regard. That God would uproot a tree or throw a mountain into the sea at the bidding of a man of faith was not inconceivable to a person of faith in an age where even pagans considered miracles to hardly be out of the ordinary. But at the same time, there must have been more than a vague awareness that a more sophisticated reinterpretation of the Bible was well underway in Alexandria and other intellectual centers of the Jewish world—a sophistication that was, no doubt, considered tantamount to being close to an infidelity by the conservative rabbis in Galilee. Both Lee and Meier underline the conservative strain of Galilean Jewry. The latter remarks (Vol. I, p.277) that such folk were not likely to be drawn to what they must have considered to be the novelties of the Pharisees, unlike the Judaism in and around Jerusalem which had to absorb the brunt of the attempts of the Antiochine empire to turn Jews into Greeks. In half-pagan Galilee, the "Galilee of the Gentiles", small enclaves, like Nazareth, could exist apart from the more pagan towns, their distinct Jewishness all the more marked precisely because of their distance from the Jewish capital. Thus it is no accident that the revitalization of Judaism after the destruction of Jerusalem and its temple, and again after the *Bar-Kochba* revolt, began in Galilee. In the meantime, pagan towns such as Sepphoris, a scarce four miles away, might seem to have never existed, except possibly as an opportunity for outside employment as far as the inhabitants of Nazareth were concerned. And as for the seaside resort of Tiberias, the "sin city" of Galilee, Jesus, like all other good Jews of his time, probably avoided it like the plague.

Still, could the young Jesus been entirely unaware of all this ferment? While there may be some reason to suspect that Jesus may have learned a bit of Greek (see Meier, I, p. 261-2) it seems unlikely that Jesus might have known much about the details of the outside world and its thought—other than perhaps being aware that the Hebrew scriptures had already been translated into Greek. Still, would he have been aware that many of its central concepts had been, reinterpreted in terms of more philosophically refined Greek concepts by the Jewish philosopher, Philo of Alexandria? We can only speculate.

At the same time, could the fact that the pharisaic movement was a largely lay-led reinterpretation of the Old Testament faith away from the temple cult and its ritual priesthood have escaped even a village boy from Galilee—even more so when an annual trip to the big city underlined these major differences? Here is where, I suspect, the young Jesus most likely became aware of a growing division within his own tradition. Certainly the difference between the opulent temple ritual, with its vested priests and legions of minor clergy, its bloody sacrifices, and the uneasy political accommodation between the hierarchy and the Roman imperial government must have contrasted sharply with the home-town synagogue with its local rabbi, its simple round of psalms and scriptural lessons. Above all, in these differences he must have begun to sense the division between these two variations within Jewish culture that became expressed, in religious party terms, as Sadducees as opposed to Pharisees. If so, one can hardly doubt what may have been going on in the mind of this precocious boy from Galilee as he sat among the teachers, "listening to them and asking them questions".

Is it possible that the boy Jesus already begun, as many teen-agers sooner or later do, to question the why and wherefore of religious belief and observance? Was he already viewing, with some distaste, the ritualism of the official temple cult with its slaughtering of multitudes of cattle and sheep, or comparing it against the more internalized piety of the various pharisaic sects?

From what we may gather from the gospels, Jesus, not unlike the prophets before him, appears to have harbored strong reservations regarding the efficacy of temple worship, even though he revered the temple as a symbol of God's abiding presence among his people. We can judge from his later remarks and criticisms, and even more by his demonstrated disdain for the legalism and sometimes outright hypocrisy of much contemporary piety, whether that of the temple or of some of the more legalistic types of phariseeism. Indeed, this might just be the motive behind Luke's recounting of this story in the first place—a 'prophecy' in a way of what is to come.

Yet all this is so much surmising and that we can say little more except to point out that the story itself again tells us that he returned to his home town and was "subject" to his parents, and that he "increased in wisdom, in stature and in favor with God and men" (Luke 2:52).

These are important statements for us, and should dispel the sort of silly speculation that some well-meaning Christians, and even some later theologians, have engaged in when they let doctrinal presuppositions, orthodox or otherwise, become more important in their minds than the gospel narratives. The obvious meaning of these passages is that Jesus, whether as an infant, child, adolescent or youth, grew and developed just the same as anyone else of his day and age. His growth was not only physical, but also mental ("in wisdom"), and spiritual ("in God's favor" or "grace") just as that of any person in his or her early life. Other than this one single incident, there is no hint of anything special about him, at least in any sense of which he was conscious. And even here, allowing for the gospel writer's hindsight, there is nothing in this story to indicate anything different than a particular precocity and giftedness marking this older boy becoming a young man. Jesus is someone who bears special watching. He will be a marked man and that to some degree he already senses it, because for him God's "business" is the same as his "Father's" business and he seems more than eager to begin his apprenticeship.

The Hidden Years: Unconventional Faith?

After this one incident, are we told nothing more about his youth and young manhood in Nazareth. If the infancy narratives have tried in some way to fill in for the absence of hard information regarding Jesus' origins, the silence of Matthew and Luke about the years that followed are even more striking. They are truly what the old "Life of Christ" type of book generally called them: "the hidden years". But still, may we not surmise some more?

If Luke's portrait of the boy-soon-to-be-man in the temple is meant to heighten an impression of individual and vocational self-awareness—certainly this must be part of what is behind Luke's words about his "father's business"—the process of coming to full self-realization must have taken many years. Whether the boy Jesus really ever said those words or not, the impact of its meaning is inescapable as we try to imagine what the self-consciousness of Jesus was as he passed from later adolescence into manhood.

In my earlier book on faith development, seeking to simplify James Fowler's terminology and his naming of the next stage of faith as "Synthetic-Conventional", I decided to rename it *"Conventional"* and leave it at that. I somewhat regret that decision now. "Conventional" can mean merely ordinary, and I doubt Jesus' own faith was ever that. If I had to choose one of the two terms now, I'd choose "synthetic" as much as I would fear that might be misunderstood as meaning "artificial". Rather, by "synthetic", Fowler meant simply that this next stage is marked by the formation of a *synthesis*, that is, the coming together of many different elements to form a new whole. Normally, what is "conventional" about such faith is that this synthesis is most apt to consist of elements taken from what is usual or normal in the environment in which it is formed, combining the ideas learned from one's parents with those learned at school and from friends and from society at large. But aside from those notional aspects, I'm not sure that the faith of the adolescent or youthful Jesus would have been judged all that typical of his peers.

As we all know, adolescence can be a time of great turmoil, one during which emotional and psychological stability can be severely tested and the quest for self-identity often takes on contradictory expressions of conformity and recalcitrance. We have no idea to what extent these moods might have affected Jesus. Pierre Babin, a French religious psychologist, saw three distinct phases to adolescence, all of them marked, to varying degrees, by a young person's attempt to define himself or herself in the face of the world, with only the final phase harboring the possibility of arriving at the threshold of a truly personal, fully-committed faith. (See Babin, 1963.)

If Jesus' own faith could be called "unconventional" during this period, it would be from a different aspect entirely, one that is more in the realm of what we would consider "psychological" than intellectual. By this I mean that the synthetic element which we would expect to be found in the otherwise conventional faith of Jesus in his adolescence may have been complicated to an unusual degree, at least for that day and age, by a crisis of self-identity. My reason for hazarding this guess, however, is not in any way based on the infancy narratives or Luke's single story about Jesus' own boyhood. My reasons are calculated from what we can know about Jesus much later on.

It has become commonplace to characterize our own age as one of extreme individualism and self-awareness, at least compared to previous periods in human history. To an extent that we find almost incomprehensible, we moderns, particularly those of us who live in the culture of the western world, seem unable to grasp the sense of solidarity, the sense of group identity that normally holds individual persons tightly in its grip in other cultures. In fact, we even find it hard to imagine how much this group mentality dominated our own ancestors' lives. For example, it has been noted that almost all the phrases or words in the English language that begin with the word or prefix "self-" are completely absent from the vocabulary of just a few centuries ago. Such current terms as "self-awareness", "self-identity", "self-determination", "self-fulfillment", etc.—these were concepts and goals that were largely unknown or ignored, or if conscious at all, usually regarded with some suspicion.

While I again realize that it is especially risky to try to delve into what the mentality of Jesus may have been in this regard, particularly at this stage of his life with so little to go on, but I suspect that where his adolescent or youthful faith may have been most unconventional was in this area of self-awareness or what the great psychiatrist Carl Jung called "individuation". The reason for my guess is again the unusual degree to which Jesus referred to God as "Father". Not only was his use of the term, for his particular culture unusual (for reasons I've already explained), but also almost outrageously personal in its tone. He taught his followers that not only God was "your [their] father" but seems to have especially referred often to God as "*My* [his] Father."

It has often been said that a major element in the process of individuation is the cutting of ties with one's parent. Freud observed that for a man, probably the greatest or most significant moment in his own self-development is the death of one's father, because even if one happens to be closer to one's mother, still, the death of one's father means, psychologically speaking, the moment when one must assume full responsibility for oneself. The same is probably true regarding a woman's relationship to her mother, although, in a more patriarchal society, probably not to the same extent. Yet, at the same time, it is usually only after a parent's death that the younger person begins to realize how much he or she owes to that parent and how dependent they were upon that person. Accepting that parent's death, then, is often the precondition to discovery of one's own true self.

What this means for one's relationship to God may be uncertain. In some cases, it appears to have no effect whatsoever, but in others, it may occasion a religious break-through. In the case of Jesus, especially if he had lost the presence of Joseph fairly early, the substitution of the sense of God's own personal fatherhood may not only have been enhanced but also have brought about, in the process, an even greater sense of self-awareness that is usual during one's youth.

I realize that all this is mere speculation, but I think there might be something to it, especially if the meaning of Luke's story about the boy Jesus in the temple is meant to be predictive—how else interpret the contrast between Joseph being called "your father" (by Mary) and the answer of Jesus who contrasts Joseph to "my father" and his own need to devote himself to His interests?

One other possible natural reason for Jesus' own degree of self-awareness suggests itself. Up to this point I have stressed the lack of sophistication of the Galilean Jews as compared to what must have been the case in Jewish culture in and around Jerusalem itself. The jibe "What good can come from Nazareth?" and the condescending remarks about Galileans in general recorded in the gospels indicate, again, that the Jews in that northern province were considered to be unenlightened, potential troublemakers, or generally, of no account. They were regarded as rural ghetto dwellers in an otherwise pagan territory.

While a ghetto mentality often makes people very narrow in their thinking, it may also occasionally have just the opposite effect. When one grows up in a world where one sees oneself as part of an embattled minority, where every situation in life is almost always seen within a mental framework of "them" against "us", there would seem to be a certain inevitable probability that at least some of the members of that society are going to strike out in a more independent direction of thought, one which to some extent is seen as a betrayal of one's own group. Chaim Potock, in his novel, *The Chosen*, described such a process in the mind of a young Orthodox Jew in New York and the effect it had of separating the young man from much of what he had known. But such a growing awareness of the wider world outside cannot be accomplished without a deeper awareness of oneself. So it must have been for Jesus in Nazareth. At least we must surmise that, even in what we think of as conventional faith, Jesus was in some marked way becoming more unconventional.

Yet the question remains: did this happen all at once, or only over a long period of time? The twenty years from early adolescence to full manhood may have remained hidden because they were outwardly unremarkable—either because they contained a faith life that was indistinguishable from those of his fellow town-folk or else because they masked a growth that was so profound that it needed the seclusion of complete anonymity to bear its fullest fruit.

There is no way that we will ever know. The Spirit that works unseen will blow where and when it will. So too is the process that marks the conversion from a merely conventional to a more intensely personal faith. For some—the "twice-born" to use William James' term—the change can be dramatic and even disorienting. For others— the "once born"—the growth can be imperceptible until it blooms full-flower. I'm inclined to think that Jesus belonged to the latter group. What was to happen alongside the Jordan was the final bursting forth of a vocation many years in the making.

Still, we can assume that outwardly his life was more or less conventional, that he did apprentice carpentry—more likely handyman work of all sorts as well as general house-building—at first under Joseph's direction and, somewhere along the line, all on his own. If he appeared unusual in any way, it may have been, and would suspect, in his devotion to God in prayer and scripture reading, and perhaps in a certain apartness that was conspicuous in his apparent reluctance to marry.

Certain recent commentators, (for example, John C. Dwyer, 1983) suggest that Jesus probably had married but childless, was either separated or widowed. This thesis, even if rather conservative compared to speculations regarding Jesus' relationship to Mary Magdalene (based mostly on later apocryphal writings as *The Gospel of Philip*) seems unwarranted as it is untraditional. Most authorities, such as Meier, who considers the question at some length (I, pp. 332-45), find it improbable. Unusual as the single life was among Jews during that period, we know far sure, on his own testimony, that the apostle Paul remained a celibate. Nor was institutional celibacy among Jews entirely unknown, as we can see from the existence of the Essenes during that same period. No doubt it would have been generally expected that Jesus would marry, but there seems to be no reason that would militate against him having postponed the decision to do so, particularly if something else may have been brewing in his mind. Again, perhaps Luke's story of the boy Jesus in the temple is meant to be a hint of some such thing.

There has been much speculation in recent years, ever since the discovery of the Dead Sea Scrolls, on what influences the Essenes may have had on Jesus' own religious consciousness. This Jewish sect may have had an influence that spread far beyond their headquarters at the monastic-like center that they maintained in the Judean desert at Qumran, just a few miles south of Jericho, on the northwest shore of the Dead Sea. Although the core members of the community appear to have lived a celibate life, there may have been married followers as well— some of who must have lived elsewhere. Ritual ablutions, or bathing, were one of the major features of their religious practice, while much of their literature speaks in apocalyptic terms of a coming divine judgment and a messiah-like deliverer who is characterized as, or is to be preceded by, an expected Teacher of Righteousness.

We shall see shortly that much of this sounds similar to what is said about John the Baptist. Could Jesus have been aware of all this way up in Galilee? It seems possible, even if no mention of these Essenes appears in the gospels—indeed, until recently we hardly knew of their existence except for a few fleeting references to them in the work of the Jewish-Roman historian, Flavius Josephus. Much still remains to be learned about them, with piles of fragmented scrolls still needing to be reconstructed and deciphered. But given the religious conservatism of the Sadduccees, fighting to retain their control in the political turmoil of the capitol, the various schools of the Pharisees, the radically nationalist Zealots and the mystical Essenes, each group espousing its own version of Judaism, Jesus, even in the hinterland town of Nazareth, must have been exposed to a bewildering variety of options.

If there is any truth to the adage that "the boy is the father of the man", then we have to conclude that the youthful Jesus must have been developing an extraordinary sense of mission, of a call toward something else than his work-a-day life as an inhabitant of a small provincial town. But what that vocation was remained to be seen. By the time he was thirty years of age or thereabouts, the urgency became clear. He must strike out on his own to the Jordan where John was baptizing and calling for a spiritual renewal among the chosen people.

Chapter 2

The Call

The movement from a merely conventional into a truly personal faith, although it often begins in late adolescence or early adulthood, often takes many years. Since we have next to no information about the hidden years of the life of Jesus in Nazareth, it is impossible to say, despite our speculations in the last chapter, just when this transition in the faith of Jesus took place. No doubt Luke's story of The Finding in the Temple might be seen as pointing towards the beginning of such a change, but when this transition was complete, is anyone's guess.

Ideally, the emergence of a fully "Individuative-reflective" faith, as Fowler has termed it—which I shall persist in calling simply a *"personal faith"*—takes place in early adulthood. Pierre Babin saw little possibility of it taking place, in any permanently committed sense, until the final stage of adolescence. But from the life stories of so many persons, even of great saints like Augustine, as well as from an accumulation of modern testimonies, we know that often such an intensely personal commitment to God comes to many only later in life, sometimes not even until the end of life. So, beginning with adulthood, and unlike the predictability of the earlier stages during childhood and adolescence, Fowler's stages of faith-development are simply a schema nothing more. Frequently real life makes a shambles of neat categories. Yet such systemization does give us hints of where to look for the signs of growth.

Generally speaking, the transition to a truly personal faith often involves a preliminary negative phase, one that includes a certain amount of testing, questioning, or outright doubt. In addition, the more positive aspect characterized by a more positive, decisive choice comes to the fore only with a sense of personal mission or vocation. Rarely does one come into a personal faith in the abstract. Faith, to the extent that it involves a basic commitment, requires that this commitment take a concrete shape in the living of one's life. Whatever we might surmise about the personal faith of Jesus of Nazareth, we really cannot begin to see the shape of its reality until a certain sense of personal mission manifests itself.

The Baptism in the Jordan

The prophet Elijah, who, according to the Bible (2 Kings 2:11), had ascended to heaven in a whirlwind, had returned in the person of John the Baptist, or so it seemed in the view of many who witnessed the burst of activity along the Jordan where the strange figure of John, clothed in a leather loincloth and a camel's hair cloak, was calling people to conversion and proclaiming the imminent arrival of the Kingdom of God.

Although both the gospels of Matthew and Luke contain infancy accounts, strictly speaking, the historical content of all four of the gospels, as well as the criteria set for that witnessing function essential to apostleship as stipulated in the Acts of the Apostles (Acts 1:22), begins here. As we have already seen, the person chosen to bear apostolic testimony must have been a witness of the words and deeds of Jesus "from the time when John was baptizing until the day he was taken up from us." Paul was to see himself as an exception, "as one born out of due time", as he was to say. Mark's gospel, which in the opinion of almost all scholars today is the earliest of the synoptic gospels, begins abruptly at this point. There is no attempt to trace Jesus' earthly beginnings. The Jesus who presents himself to history is a grown man who suddenly appears along the banks of the Jordan.

So too the Gospel of John, whose famous prologue is primarily a theological meditation. The actual narrative or story line, beginning with verse 19 of Chapter 1, flows directly from the testimony of John the Baptist in verse 15. The events that took place at that time stand almost alone—along with the story of Jesus' passion and death, as well as the different accounts attesting to his resurrection—as being singled out for mention in all four of the gospels. So clearly we have here an event of the greatest importance for our understanding of Jesus.

Despite the importance of this first public appearance of Jesus, there is a curious discrepancy regarding the memory of Jesus' own baptism itself. John alone among the evangelists doesn't recount the actual event but, also alone among them, indicates that Jesus and his own disciples performed the baptismal rite on others (see John 3:22) mimicking John the Baptist and his disciples—among whom had once been this "beloved disciple" himself. The situation here is not unlike that regarding the Last Supper narratives and the Eucharist. John alone, again, does not recount the action or the words of institution over the bread and wine. Instead, there is the long discourse on Jesus' body and blood as our "food and drink" in chapter six, but with a concluding emphasis on not the flesh but the spirit giving eternal life. In much the same way, the theologies of rebirth and illumination replace the account of baptism as such in John's gospel.

What we see here, according to scholars such as Meier, who devotes three whole chapters to the subject of John the Baptist and his relationship to Jesus and his ministry, is a manifestation of a later rivalry between the disciples of John and those of Jesus. This was a rivalry that the followers of Jesus, despite the historical record, wished to avoid, especially by playing down the implication that Jesus in any way needed to be baptized. There are hints of this attitude in Matthew's gospel as well. Although all four gospels claim that Jesus indeed is the one whom John predicted as "the one yet to come ... whose sandals I am not worthy to untie" and who will "baptize with the Holy Spirit and fire", it is only Matthew's gospel that attempts to meet the problem head-on by having the baptizer protest to Jesus before he baptizes him; "It is I who need baptism from you...", with Jesus replying, "Leave it like this for the time being; it is fitting that we should, in this way, do all that righteousness demands" (Matthew 3:14-15).

Like John's silence regarding Jesus himself undergoing baptism, this Matthean explanation was already struggling with the conflict between the followers of the Baptist and those of Jesus. While there can be no doubt that this same struggle is reflected in Mark and Luke, there is no hedging or apology for Jesus having undergone John's penitential rite. He submits to it like any of the rest of John's disciples or followers.

In doing this, Jesus sets himself apart from the crowd of the curious, both the mere sightseers as well as the suspicious, some of which have been sent as spies from the political-religious establishment in Jerusalem. We must not overlook, at this point, the extremely precarious political implications of the baptizer's message. The Jewish nation was a captive people and what little political authority was still held by Jews under the Roman occupation was mostly, with the exception of the brief reign (AD 40-44) of Herod Agrippa, under the canon of religious affairs. Any religious reform, such as John the Baptist preached, threatened this remaining political influence and seemed perilously close to the open revolt advocated by the Zealots. These political implications were to contribute greatly to, and in fact were probably the real reason for, the death of John the Baptist (according to Meier, who finds the account given by the Jewish historian Josephus as more reliable than that reported in the Gospels). They could not have been less than a warning to Jesus himself.

Nevertheless, there can be no doubt, from the evidence given by the synoptic gospels and the Acts of the Apostles (see especially the kerygmatic addresses of Peter and Paul in Acts 10:37ff. and 13:24ff.), that the baptism of Jesus by John in the Jordan was seen by the evangelists as the occasion when the mission of Jesus began, for it was then that according to all four Gospels, that:

> The heavens opened up and the Spirit, as a dove, descended ... and from the heavens a voice said, "You are my Son, the Beloved: my favor rests on you."

Although the above quotation has been taken from Mark 1:10-11, with slight variations in the wording of this account in the parallel synoptic passages (Matt. 3:16-17; Luke 3:22) as well as in John 1:33b-34, the sense in all the accounts is the same: Jesus is revealed to be God's "beloved Son".

Two questions should immediately come to mind. What is to be made of this revelation? And to whom is it made?

Commentators have long noted that the phrase "the beloved, in whom I am well pleased", evokes the passage in Isaiah 42:1, the first of the four so-called "Suffering Servant" songs (see Isaiah 42:1-4; 49:1-6; 50:4-11; 52:13-53:12). The connection here to Isaiah also is subtly underlined when it is realized that in the Aramaic dialect that John the Baptist undoubtedly used, the word *talya* that meant "lamb", also meant "servant" (see footnote "c" to Isaiah 53:7 in *The New Jerusalem Bible*). Hence we have the "Lamb of God" allusion in John's description of this event as well (see John 1:29).

Add to this that although the Greek texts of the synoptic gospels use the more explicit word *huios* for "son", it is more than merely a coincidence that the word *pais*, which the ancient Greek Septuagint version uses to serve as a translation of the Hebrew *ebed* or "servant" in its version of Isaiah, also can mean "son" in Greek. This same understanding of the Greek word *pais* is also found in one of the earliest Christian catechetical books, the *Didache* or "The Teaching of the Twelve Apostles", where Jesus is described as God's *"pais"*. If nothing can be proved directly by this close association of the two meanings for *pais* in Greek, we can see from this, along with the supposed Aramaic connection between "lamb" and "servant", that early Christianity had early on made a direct connection between these famous Isaian passages and Christianity's own claim that Jesus is indeed the "Son of God". The importance of these connections will become more evident in time, but for now let it stand to underline the mysterious prophetic content of the baptismal accounts.

Beside the question of the meaning of these words, the other question still remains as to whom are they pictured as first having been revealed? Obviously, taken as a "second level" (that of early Christian *kerygma*) the idea is to reveal this fact to the reader of these accounts. But as far as to whom the revelation is supposed to have been made at the time it occurred, the testimony is mixed. According to Matthew and Mark, it is apparently only Jesus himself who saw or heard anything. Luke, on the other hand, does not specify whom the hearer or hearers might be. John's gospel departs from the others not only in totally ignoring the fact of Jesus having been baptized, but even more in singling out the Baptist as later testifying that he himself was granted the vision of "the Spirit coming down from heaven upon him and resting upon him." (See John 1:32. Here the phrase "like a dove" seems to have been borrowed from the synoptic accounts and is missing in some early manuscripts of John.)

Nevertheless, it appears that in Matthew and Mark, in particular, the emphasis remains on the experience that Jesus himself had. No doubt it is Luke's account, which fails to specify the recipient of the words and vision, that has inspired later efforts to reinterpret this whole event as a Trinitarian theophany where the Father (the voice from heaven) reveals the Son (Jesus) through the visible sign of the Spirit (the Dove)—this for the edification of all who were standing around.

As to be expected, with his crusade against any psychologizing type of "lives of Jesus", Meier denies (II, p. 107) that this theophany mirrors any inner experience that Jesus may have had, but simply reflects the desire of the early Church to define, from the outset of the gospels, the real identity of Jesus and to set him apart from any counter-claims from followers of John. Yet even Meier has to admit that this whole episode may very well signify a turning-point in the relationship of Jesus to John, one at which Jesus began to realize that he had a distinct mission that set him apart from his mentor.

So it would appear that in a manner somewhat similar to early "adoptionist" christology, as well as many modern commentators, we might see in this event—that is, his baptism, as apart from any visionary experiences—a clear sign that it was only at this point that Jesus became aware of his mission and his special relationship to God. Leaving aside the question of what his "sonship" means, this certainly seems to be an interpretation that is much more in line with an understanding of a Jesus who is fully human. Even in the Johannine version, this approach is not precluded; it is only, at the most, downplayed.

Nevertheless, I feel that this also may be an oversimplification of the matter. Such an interpretation almost entirely overlooks what immediately follows in the synoptic gospels. Instead of the force of this event launching Jesus immediately into missionary activity, as we might expect, according to the synoptic gospels something quite the contrary took place. We are told "immediately, the Spirit drove him into the desert" (Mark 1:12), to which Matthew (4:1) adds, "to be tempted by the devil."

The Temptations in the Desert

If no event depicted by the gospels seems as clearly historical, taken at face value, as his baptism, its aftermath, presented by the synoptic gospels, presents the most puzzling of all the other major episodes recorded of him. Again, John's gospel chooses to remain silent about the whole thing. Even the relative sparsity of biblical commentary on this subject (Meier devotes only two pages to the matter; half of page 103 in the second volume of his immense work with a page-and-a-half footnote on pages 271-2) seems to reduplicate in a new way the serious uneasiness in traditional thought over how to incorporate this aspect of the gospel into the body of Christian orthodoxy.

The reason for this modern reticence is, of course, the patently dramatic and visionary nature of the accounts. Even if they actually happened, who else would have been there to witness them? As in the theophany reported in conjunction with his baptism, who can say, in terms of historical argument, that anything else happened at all? Yet even Meier has to admit that the "criterion of multiple attestation"—with the exception of John's non-synoptic gospel—argues strongly that Jesus did retreat to the desert for a period of time immediately following his baptism and that there he underwent some kind of "inner spiritual struggle in preparation for his public ministry" (Meier II, p. 272). This admission, for the purposes of this book, is more than sufficient.

Nevertheless, reflecting the silence of the Gospel of John, the concept of Jesus being tempted in the first place seems shocking to many Christian minds. Recall the outrage over Martin Scorcese's film of Nikos Kazantzakis' novel, *The Last Temptation of Christ.* (Even Kazantzakis seems to have had problems in trying to portray these particular temptations, if not all the others he imagined.) On the other hand, the most ancient commentaries play up the theme of Jesus having gone into the desert to show his future adversary who is in charge—not unlike St. Anthony of Egypt and the other ancient Christian desert fathers who went into solitude to defeat Satan in one-to-one combat. Of course, in such a scenario, there is no question as to who is going to win!

But instead of a picture of Jesus rushing into the desert to do battle with the adversary, the synoptic gospels approach the story with a quite different note. According to Mark, who gives the shortest, and presumably earliest account, Jesus was even "driven" into the desert by "the spirit" while Matthew and Luke soften the expression to his being "led" into the desert. Only Luke assures us that this was the Holy Spirit—although we can presume from Mark and Matthew's way of phrasing things that it is not the devil's impulse that took him there. There, Matthew tells us, Jesus "fasted for forty days and forty nights" and that "afterwards" (Luke is not so specific as to the time) he was "tempted".

Although Mark does not tell us what these temptations were, Matthew and Luke are explicit and picture to us three separate temptations, differing only in the order of the last two. For reasons that I will explain shortly, and contrary to Meier's reasoning on this matter—his based, it would seem, more on a hierarchy of sin—I will use the order of Luke's account here (see Luke 4:1-13).

The first temptation, certainly the logical one after a forty-day fast, is to "command that this stone become a loaf of bread." Note that in Luke 4:3 there is only one stone. Although perhaps we shouldn't attach any particular significance to this, it could possibly point to a more individualistic self-serving temptation, which is to say, is to satisfy Jesus' own hunger. In contrast, the Matthean version, with its plurality of stones/loaves, seems to underscore the populist appeal of any messianic miracle-working, not so much to quell Jesus' own hunger, but to present himself as a new Moses, providing an imagined future audience with a new *manna* in the desert. However, in either case Jesus quotes scripture (Deuteronomy 8:3) to dispel this temptation, with Matthew adding a final emphasis on the "word of God".

The second temptation, according to Luke's presentation, is that Jesus might gain dominion over the entire world, by one act alone—simply by worshiping the Tempter. Jesus' response is curt. It is another quote from Deuteronomy (6:13): "You shall worship the Lord your God and him alone shall you serve." But this time it is Luke who stresses the messianic dimensions of the temptation. Where Matthew's account holds out simply the promise of "all the kingdoms of the world and their glory" (Matthew. 4:8), in Luke this is elaborated into "all the kingdoms of the world in a moment of time" and not only that, but "all this authority and their glory, for it has been delivered to me"—suggesting an allusion to the authority of imperial Rome. Accordingly, this is may not be so much a simple appeal to worship Satan, but rather an appeal to worship the ungodly power of evil embodied in the state. If so, then here the overtones closely parallel the picture of idolatry presented in the book of Revelations.

Lastly, the third temptation—at least in the Luke's order that we are following—pictures Jesus as then being transported to the pinnacle of the temple in Jerusalem where he is tempted to test God directly, this time by putting his fate directly in God's hands, with the Tempter quoting from Psalm 91. Thus Jesus is bidden to "throw himself down" to be rescued by God's angels. But Jesus again answers from Deuteronomy (6:16): "You must not put the Lord your God to the test."

My reason for following the order given by Luke is not to ease the problem of credibility involved by transporting Jesus to Jerusalem and back. Even traditional Christians have taken these temptations to be patently symbolic or visionary—how else do you see all the world's kingdoms in a moment? As for the purpose of throwing himself down, any nearby cliff (of which there are many in the Judean desert) would have sufficed. But if we follow the order given by Luke, the idea that this temptation was really encountered in a visit to Jerusalem, where the corner of the temple balustrade presents a precipitous drop to the Kedron Valley below, presents much less of a problem. This is more likely if a visit to Jerusalem, as depicted by John shortly after the meeting with John the Baptist, did take place at that time. But at this point the question of the physical circumstances is not that important. What is important is the actual meaning.

It is noteworthy that the first and last temptation, in the order given by Luke, both begin with the phrase "If you are the Son of God..." In the case of the other temptation (the second as described by Luke), however, the implication is that he is really not divine, but that he can gain its equivalence by worshipping the proffered source of earthly power. The usual explanation given for all this is that while Jesus surely knew himself to be the Son of God, it was the devil that really wasn't so sure. But this is an interpretation that appears to contradict all the other statements in the gospels about the evil spirits proclaiming Jesus' identity—but of course, only after Jesus had been tested in this way.

Again, I read the whole episode quite differently. Instead, to revert to modern psychological jargon, I would suggest that what we have here are all the indications needed to describe of an actual identity crisis.

However outrageous this suggestion may seem, I invite the reader to try to imagine the following scenario.

Jesus, responding to his best instincts and to the prompting of the Spirit, after years of seclusion in Nazareth, went to the Jordan to be initiated into the revival movement of John, only to be given the revelation (or should we say "hit with the realization"?) that God had singled out himself, Jesus, not John, with the special mission of inaugurating the kingdom. John, if we are to believe his own testimony as recorded by all four gospels, saw himself only as a herald, a precursor, "a voice crying in the wilderness". But instead of joining John as an ally, Jesus had suddenly experienced the overwhelming power of the conviction that he must go beyond John. He must begin the implementation or embodiment of that kingdom or reign of God in its actuality, not just in its promise.

What did or does this word "kingdom" mean? That, first of all, was the obvious problem—as we can see from the later confusion of his disciples. Was it to be constituted by an open revolt against Rome, as the Zealots would urge? Or was it to be a sudden Day of Judgment, as John the Baptist's preaching seemed to foretell. Or could it be simply a reform of his people's religion as such, perhaps through a purging of the corruption surrounding the temple worship combined with a more spiritual reinterpretation of the Law as many of the Pharisees were urging. These were all possibilities to be considered and with which he must wrestle.

Yet this was only the operative or strategic side of the question. The deeper, more essential, side was who he himself might be. To be designated God's "Servant-Son" could mean very different things in these different contexts. To be a "Messiah" as the Zealots imagined him would be one thing, while to be a "Teacher of Righteousness" whom the Essenes and, presumably, the Pharisee's might have also followed, would be quite another. And, in addition, there was also the mysterious, enigmatic "Son of Man", the shadowy apocalyptic figure who appears in the prophecies of Daniel, the vision of whom may have inspired John the Baptist's warnings of a judgment to come. In other words, the message itself determined the mission and identity of its proclaimer. If, as Albert Schweitzer and his disciples said, "Jesus proclaimed the kingdom, and his followers proclaimed Jesus", this need not be taken as an unwarranted presumption. It is the ultimate guarantee of the authenticity of God's word. Or in this case especially, as a pundit of a later age would proclaim, "The medium is the message."

That may have very well been the problem that drove Jesus, under the impulse of the Spirit, into the desert. Like another Elijah, John the Baptist had emerged from the desert to proclaim God's word. Now, almost like a second reincarnation of Elijah, Jesus is driven back into the desert, and like the first Elijah as he moved toward Mt. Horeb in the footsteps of Moses to seek God's will, Jesus secludes himself in the desert to confront for the first time that disturbing question: "Who do men say that I am?"

Up to this point, despite what has been said about the process of individuation and the effect it may have had upon his self-consciousness, it may be safe to say that Jesus, as far as we can know from the gospels, apart from what may have only been idle speculation on our part, may have had little sense of himself as an individual in any way different from any pious Jew of his age. Even if we were to keep turning back to Luke's depiction of the incident known as "The Finding in the Temple" as indicative of a certain precocity, and we were to take that episode as somehow recalling the actual words of Jesus, the sheer ingenuousness of the answer of the boy to his parents seems to indicate that he really saw nothing extraordinary about his relationship to God. After all, why should his parents, of all people, pious Jews that they were, worry about him or see anything unusual about his eagerness to learn? Instead, it is the Evangelist who plays up a deeper meaning of the word "father" and his parent's bewildered surprise.

No doubt, Jesus had listened carefully to the rabbis and other scholars and pious men who had come his way. To some extent, despite all the negative things said about them in the gospels, it might be said that Jesus loosely identified himself with the beginnings of that reform movement generally known as "phariseeism". Although the great variety of opinions over biblical interpretation and the various approaches to piety current in the society of that time make it difficult to categorize Jesus as being an adherent of any one particular school or tradition, Professor David Flusser, of Hebrew University, Jerusalem, considered to be the Jewish expert on the New Testament, believes that Jesus can be tentatively associated with one particular pharisaic group, which Flusser identifies as being "the Pharisees of Love".

But there can also be no question that Jesus definitely did not in any way identify with the would-be Jewish ruling elite in Jerusalem, known as the Sadducees, even though he retained a critical respect for the temple ceremonies which these establishment types still controlled and often demeaned in their concern to capitalize on the piety of the average Jew. But perhaps Jesus did think that there was something that he, even as one small, unimportant, relatively uneducated but well-meaning person from the provinces might do? It may be that, to his mind, the Pharisees were too divided among themselves to effect any major reform.

No doubt, news of the strong stand being taken by John along the Jordan must have filtered its way up to Nazareth. Jesus went down to witness what was taking place and in turn, offered his own life completely to the service of God—indeed; this was the whole point of John's baptism in its demand for conversion. What is different about Jesus, as compared to the rest of John's followers, is that Jesus is not only taken at his word, but that he is also declared to be God's "Servant-Son". What this declaration might mean, and the mission this implied, is the question, but not the final answer, which the temptations in the desert underline.

Before this, it must have been different. Certainly Jesus knew himself to be a "child" or a "servant" of God, and even a "son of God" in the sense that he knew that Jews, as members of a chosen people, were called to be special in God's eyes. Even more, his extraordinary devotion to God as *Abba* or "Father" speaks eloquently of his sense of closeness to God, a closeness that cannot but reflect favorably on his home and childhood. But now, perhaps for the first time, in all its stark reality, Jesus knew that he is truly different. It could be that he felt something like the volunteer who, thinking he might help in some way in a mission, suddenly finds himself designated as "Chief" or commander of the whole operation. Who knows? But whatever his feelings, it is obvious that he fled to the desert to find the answer to what he was really being called to be.

The choices were limited. He could attempt the route of the Zealots—to foment a popular revolution, to turn "stone(s)" to "bread", as we are told he turned a few loaves into a camp meal on more than one occasion and was almost drafted into leadership. Not only stones to bread, the stony resignation of his people under centuries of repression he knew could also be transformed into a mob of impassioned liberators who could throw out not only the Roman oppressors, but their rich and powerful allies among the Jews as well. To be "*the* Son of God"—would this not be to become the Liberator, the Messiah of Israel?

Or, on the other hand, if he were not the "Son of God"—even in the sense of God's chosen agent—yet still desired to further the reform and freedom of Israel, would it not be a wiser move to somehow ally oneself with the forces of oppression to reform them from within; or as another age would say: "if you can't beat them, join them"? Maybe, in this way, some providential opportunity would present itself that could be used to turn the situation around entirely. Yet, would not such a course of action be an idolatry of power, a going over to Satan in the self-deluding hope that he could turn Satan's power against evil?—a temptation worth pondering, no doubt, but in the end deceptive. At best it would be an immoral course, no matter, how noble the intentions. Worldly power, in the end, cannot serve God's real purposes, and those who think it can have already prostrated themselves before a false god.

Is there any other way out? Perhaps there is: this is why I'm inclined to think that the order of the temptations as presented by Luke rings more true, at least psychologically speaking. One can put things entirely in God's hands. This, the final possibility or resolution, however, can also be the final temptation. Could it be that Jesus, driven to despair to find an answer, was tempted to find it, to force God's hand as it were, by throwing himself over a cliff? Or like the prophet Elijah before him, who in the desert prayed that God would take his life (I Kings 19:4) or the prophet Jeremiah who came to rue the day he'd been born (Jeremiah 20:14-18) that already the burden of the message and ministry that confronted Jesus was in danger of proving too much for him? Who is to say, if Jesus truly was a man, that such a temptation was impossible? Indeed, later in his ministry, when he spoke enigmatically of "going to" somewhere "where you can't follow", his listeners even wondered if he was intending to kill himself (see John 8:22). So at least the possibility of suicide was not beyond his hearers' imagination. The intensity of the prophetic ministry is not without its recognized dangers!

Be that as it may, the temptation, as presented in the gospels, is not that far-fetched. Even the topography suggests it. If this temptation did not actually take place at the temple, then the location of the monastery of the Quadrantine (the "Forty Days") that is perched on a cliff face overlooking the site of ancient Jericho and the Jordan Valley and Dead Sea beyond, is a fitting enough place to recall this and those other solitaries who have gone mad in the desert.

Might not this final temptation have taken place at the temple in Jerusalem after all? A long day's hike (from the desert above Jericho), uphill all the way, but half-starved and feverish from the dryness and heat of the desert, could not have Jesus' quandary between the way of popular revolt and the way of political influence have possibly driven him to seek a solution, no longer in the wilderness, where he found no answer, but in the midst of the capitol and it's holiest place? The temple was, of all things, that which most of all symbolized the reformation that was needed, and also the place where the powers that be, no matter how subservient to the foreigners, still had the influence to bring about change, if they wanted it—which they did not. What better place for a final contest, not with those powers so much, or even with the mob, but with himself, and with God? Jesus would wrest, if he could, an answer from God or else die in the attempt. What more decisive a resolution could there be? How could he not be tempted by it?

But the answer was not to come yet, at least not that day and not that way. Perhaps it was the sight of the temple itself in all its near-completed magnificence—this was the third one on this spot and would be the grandest of them all. Or maybe it was the sight of all these people, especially all these little, sincere and devout people who streamed to the temple all day long to hand over their pathetic, over-priced offerings. Or maybe it was even the sight of the foreign tourists and soldiers who for all their affected disdain were underneath impressed and even awed by the majesty of this great monument to Israel's God. Or could there have been a premonition that the showdown would come another day in another way, close by these same city and temple walls and that the moment of truth must be according to the Father's own choosing?

If Jesus did cause a stir in the temple shortly after his baptism, as the second chapter of John's gospel indicates, it apparently didn't amount to much—or else the authorities chose to ignore it. In any case, Jesus must have come away with the conviction that he must wait for God, not tempt him, and that the time would come soon enough when he would have to challenge the authorities at this august spot, not by a spectacular, or even suicidal leap, but by some calculated action that God would reveal to him before long. So Jesus found his way back to his home province and to his hometown. The meaning of his "Sonship", it was clear by now, was to be in the pattern of the Isaian "Servant of *Jahweh*" and the suffering that would entail.

Jesus and Personal Faith

What we have here, in these combined stories of the baptism and the temptations of Jesus is, I would submit, (despite my wondering, in the previous chapter, as to whether the faith of Jesus was ever "conventional" in the usual sense of that word) is a definitive movement from what generally corresponds to conventional faith to a more intensely personal faith. By contemporary standards, and by much of what I have implied, we may have the impression that a conventional faith, because it is conventional and highly influenced by family, society, and culture in general, is an inferior type of faith. In some ways it is—especially if we look at it from the aspect of personal resolution or conviction on a purely intellectual level. But we must make no mistake about confusing that with lack of genuine commitment or holiness. If the faith of Jesus had been somewhat conventional in terms of what was then contemporary Judaism until around his thirtieth year, we must realize that for him or anyone like him in his society, although there was plenty of variety in the expression of Judaism, still, when reduced to its basics, there was no doctrinal alternative. What little popular paganism he was exposed to must have seemed ludicrous or bizarre. But there is no doubt that at the same time Jesus must have been resolved to find an even better way of being a Jew. In this context, that he sought out the baptizer along the Jordan speaks for itself.

But what he found and he himself became was something very different from what he had left behind in Nazareth. That month and a half or so Jesus spent along the Jordan and in the near-by desert was to profoundly change him. Whatever it was that happened to him at the time of his baptism, it propelled him into a prolonged period of solitude to wrestle with its meaning. And the outcome of this test does not seem to have been completely resolved even then. Nor should this surprise us. The movement from conventional to a fully personal faith is generally not a smooth one, indeed, it is apt to be even more traumatic within closed and more or less homogeneous religious cultures—although Jewish culture at that time was rapidly ceasing to be as rigid as we may imagine it to have been or even as it was to become in later times from place to place. The broad division between Sadducees and Pharisees and the many divisions within the latter, or of revolutionary resistance groups like the Zealots or esoteric conclaves like the Essenes, all point to an amazing pluralism even within the Judaism of that time.

However, to the north, in Galilee, away from Judaism's religious and cultural capitol in Jerusalem, or its most cosmopolitan intellectual center in Alexandria, Jesus' own impression of his faith was likely to be to some extent more traditional than that of many other Jews of his time. "Personalization" or "individuation" within this religious context was primarily a matter of finding ones own special vocation within the context of a faith long received. The type of synthesis that goes on within the earlier conventional stage is much less likely to have been in evidence in the Galilean Judaism of the first century of our era. If anything, instead of the broadening synthesis that often, but not always, takes place when faith becomes personalized in our own situation, the reflection and insight that Jesus gained during this brief but decisive period in his life could be seen primarily as counter-synthetic, breaking down whatever easy accommodations may have been made between religion and society and instead demanding a radical renewal of faith.

Or to look at it from another perspective, that given by Pierre Babin, we might say that Jesus underwent a religious conversion experience in the true biblical sense of the word, a *metanoia* (literally, a "change of mind") which is not so much that of "repentance"—the usual translation given to John's message and baptism—as it is an upheaval in one's whole way of thinking or attitude towards life. Such conversions do not necessarily involve a change in religion or religious affiliation, although that also occasionally happens. What it does involve, if it is genuine, is a new deepening of one's religious commitment, one that is often expressed in a sense of mission, call or vocation, that demands a whole new manner of life. It would have been the kind of turning-point that even such a no-nonsense critic as Meier admits must have happened about this time. In Jesus' case, this sense of a "call" and its demand for a life lived with a sense of a divinely given mission is clearly evident.

In terms of risk and the threat it poses to security, this period must have been singularly traumatic for Jesus. To leave home, as humble as it was, and to venture out to follow a charismatic prophet in the wilderness, could hardly have been approached in the spirit of mere diversion on the one hand, or simply as a religious pilgrimage on the other. To lay aside his familiar tools, the simple comforts of hearthside and his mother's cooking, or even the reassuring security of well-used scrolls in the local synagogue and to be prepared to take up a wanderer's life in the footsteps of a wild-looking man who reputedly lived on grasshoppers and by raiding wild beehives could not have sounded very attractive.

On the other hand, to throw all aside to follow this man and to have to risk disappointment or disillusionment and to find oneself with no alternative but to return home wiser but sadder to a small town, where everyone knew everyone else's business, would not be an attractive prospect either. That Jesus appeared to do just that after his sojourn along the Jordan did not go unnoticed. True, he was soon to reassert his newfound call as a traveling *rabbi*, with even a small coterie of followers. But even by this time there were people, particularly among his relatives, who thought him to be somewhat unhinged (see Mark 3:21). To be different, or even to dare to be so, is to earn scorn from those who think they already know everything about you. Had they had any idea of what went on in his mind when he had been in the desert a short time back they would have been more suspicious yet. Either way, there was now no turning back.

Chapter 3

The Mission in Galilee

In almost all accounts of the life of Jesus, it is customary to divide his relatively short public ministry between the initial period in Galilee and the later culmination of events in Judea and Jerusalem. However the matter is not quite that simple. For one, there is not any unanimous agreement on just how long this public life lasted—whether it was a bit more than two years, or only little more than a year. Jesus appears to have made several trips to Jerusalem during this period, usually at the time of the major religious feasts, particularly on the Passover. However, here we run into a discrepancy, the synoptic gospels mention only two such festivals during this period, yet John's gospel seeming to indicate three.

This problem of chronology may seem purely academic, except that, for our present purposes, it presents a crucial problem of interpretation, especially hinging on the question of when Jesus actually went to Jerusalem to challenge the temple authorities. Kurt Aland's *Synopsis of the Four Gospels* opts for seeing Jesus' "cleansing of the temple" episode as described in the second chapter of John's gospel as having happened before the Galilean ministry as an alternative to placing it just after his triumphal entry into Jerusalem at the beginning of the final week of his life. Certainly, if the third temptation as depicted by Luke actually did take place at the temple, then the earlier date for this confrontation seems more likely. But all three of the synoptic gospels put it at the much later date.

Or might Jesus have raised such a ruckus in the temple on more than one occasion? I will go on the supposition, one used by the much older *Chronological Harmony of the Gospels* (Stephen J. Hartdegen, 1942) that Jesus indeed may have in fact done this at least twice. For a man with a sense of mission, it does not seem impossible. Thus we would have his early ministry in Galilee prefaced by this first attempt to cleanse the temple in Jerusalem, and his later ministry, in Judea, culminated by another episode of temple cleansing, one that would immediately lead to his passion and death.

Proceeding on these assumptions—three Passovers, two temple cleansings, and two years plus some months of public ministry—I think it is also possible to paint in broad strokes, not only a general shift of location in

Jesus' public ministry, but a shift in emphasis that represents, in a concrete way, a further transformation of Jesus' own sense of mission, and with it, a further transformation in his faith. More exactly, these changes represent, in my estimation, a distinctive shift from a faith that is deeply and intensely personal to a more fully integrated or "conjunctive" faith.

To understand this change, we have to first examine, however briefly, that first year of preaching in Galilee and the crisis to which it led.

Signs and Wonders

The mission of Jesus in Galilee was conducted in the manner of a wandering teacher or rabbi with a small group of intimate disciples or "learners"—of whom the gospels give the number as being seventy-two—along with (or including?) twelve specially chosen men who later became known as his "apostles" or "emissaries". The distinctive message of Jesus at this time centers on the theme of the "Kingdom" or "Reign of God".

A great deal of paper and ink has been expended, especially in recent times, in the attempt to explain exactly what it was that Jesus meant by this phrase. Meier devotes over two-hundred pages of his second volume to this question alone. Although the idea that Israel itself was the object of God's special providence and rule is an old one in the Hebrew bible, the actual phrase, whether in the form of "God's kingdom" or "Reign of God" or in the form favored by Matthew ("kingdom of heaven") is relatively unique to the gospels. It first appears, but only fleetingly, once in the deutereocanonical Book of Wisdom (10:10), a few times more in some of the late intra-testamental "apocrypha" or "pseudepigraphal" literature like the Psalms of Solomon and in a couple of the Qumran documents. Then the theme more or less disappears, even in the New Testament. St. Paul used the phrase only a half a dozen times or so and the other epistles even less. Even the book of Revelation, despite so much of it being devoted to the final age of God's judgment on human history, seldom uses the phrase as such.

Perhaps there is a special reason for this. The phrase itself, for all its evocative power, seems to have a rather elusive meaning. As we see it introduced in the preaching of John the Baptist, God's kingdom seems to be something that is *soon* to arrive, but *not yet* here. Its arrival will bring on the judgment of God upon Israel and bring to a close all human history. The message is unmistakably eschatological, in the sense of dealing with the final or last age, breathing very much the apocalyptic atmosphere, if not necessarily repeating the exact style, of much of this later Old Testament era literature.

On the other hand, as reportedly used by Jesus, the phrase seems to acquire a much more immediate meaning, as if it were referring to something that has *already*, to some extent, become realized in our midst. Although it is soon to make an even more definitive appearance, it is even *now* present in seminal form in the good news of God's unconditional gift of love. It is, to use some other phrases much relied upon by theologians today when discussing this subject, a "both-and" proposition, a case of the kingdom being both "imminent" (not yet, but soon, to arrive) and "realized" (already—even if not yet apparent). How much of Jesus' message is to be interpreted in either mode remains a hot topic of debate.

Just to take one example: the question of how the famous saying found in Luke 17: 21 is to be translated. According to this passage, the Pharisees asked Jesus when the kingdom of God is coming. He is said to have answered that it "is in your midst"—in the sense that it is already here. But as Meier points out (II, p. 424) this is only one possible translation. It also could mean, in an imminently future sense, that the kingdom "is within your reach"—even if not quite here yet. The only thing that it doesn't mean is that "the kingdom of God is *within* you", especially in an individualistic way. (While Jerome used the Latin *intra* to translate the Greek *entos,* he used the plural *vos* when it comes to the "you".)

In Meier's estimation, such a complete interiorization of the kingdom is almost completely at odds with rest of the "canonical Gospels in general or Luke in particular" and is a "foreign intrusion" typical of "2nd-century Christian Gnosticism" and of "19th-century German liberal Protestantism and some 20th-century American quests for the historical Jesus." His reference here seems to be to the already controversial product of the so-called "Jesus Seminar" published under the title *The Five Gospels* (Macmillan, 1993) in which the fifth is "The Gospel of Thomas". This long-lost Gnostic document, rediscovered in 1945, has influenced a few scholars, like John Dominic Crossan, whose work, *The Historical Jesus: The Life of a Mediterranean Jewish Peasant*, contains some insights into the background of Jesus that are as intriguing as his book's subtitle, but whose conclusions are hardly within the middle range of accepted scholarly opinions.

The reason for this excursion into the infighting of present-day scripture scholars is not a minor one. Apart from the historical importance of how this "Kingdom of God" is to be understood (to take two extremes, an imperial church seeing itself as the Kingdom of God on earth versus an isolated non-conformist body of believers who are convinced that the world is about to end) we also have here, in a kind of test-case example, the question of what Jesus himself may have believed. To some extent, I think all the experts would agree that Jesus did go beyond the message of John the Baptist in stressing God's forgiveness and love. But as to the question as to how and when this new reign of love and forgiveness would be manifested, they remain divided, even as we do, to some extent, within ourselves.

Back to Jesus. Did he himself think the world, or at least it's prior history to the advent of a messiah, was about to end? If so, then a great deal more of his message, not the least of which was his seeming indifference to the political situation and his apparent willingness to console people in a way that some see to be excessively passive in the face of injustice. From this foreshortened view of the future, his "Blessed are the poor ... the meek ... those who suffer persecution", etc., seems quite logical. Or on the other hand, if the "Kingdom" is entirely within—which it isn't—such passivity could equally result, but at least Jesus couldn't be accused of a complete misreading of the future. But the fact that the political and religious establishment of his time reacted as it did, and that he seems to have been aware of this probable outcome, would lead one to assume that Jesus was intending neither apocalyptic fanaticism nor pie-in-the-sky mysticism.

If the former was particularly the view of Albert Schweitzer who early in the twentieth-century gave up, all too soon it seems, on his quest for the historical Jesus, since then a great more has been learned about the Essenes and other apocalyptic currents of Jesus' time. In contrast to such groups, the teaching of Jesus seems remarkably free from exaggerations in this direction, even if it does seem to share some of the eschatological urgency of John the Baptist's theme. How to interpret this tendency, however, remains a problem. Trying to just ignore it, or deciding beforehand, that passages in the gospels that seem to reflect this line of thinking can't be authentic—which seems to have been one of the criteria used by the "Jesus Seminar"—then we do have a problem, that is, unless we drop our assumptions that Jesus couldn't have been wrong about anything.

On the other hand, suppose Jesus was really preaching an advent of a divine rule that was imminent, at least in the sense of something that could soon be realized in the form of a new era in human relationships both on a person-to-person level as well with ramifications in the whole structure of society, including its religious aspects. Then we may have an ancient form of "liberation theology", regardless whether Jesus was aware of such implications or not. But if this is the case, then the message of Jesus also differs from the pharisaic schools that saw the reign of righteousness to consist primarily in the observance of the Law (seen primarily in terms of religious piety) on the one hand and from the outright revolutionary political activism promoted by the Zealots on the other. The Kingdom of

God, in that case, would be primarily what we ask for when we pray in the words attributed to him—that our own conduct here on earth reflect that decreed by our Father in heaven. If that program were carried out, this world would indeed be a better place.

Did Jesus really believe that the world was about to end? Later, when we examine the words attributed to him about the fall of Jerusalem, we will have to take a closer look at this question. But even if Jesus thought the end of the world was imminent, he apparently did not let it affect his conviction that something more than personal repentance was required and that some reform of society was in order, at least within the community of Israel. But at the same time Jesus does not present any program of reform. His "beatitudes" may show great sympathy and understanding for the poor and oppressed, but he does not appear to have preached any type of external revolution. So despite all warnings about mistranslations, Jesus' appeal seems to have been directed first of all, like those of most of the prophets, to an interior transformation, to a change of "heart". Whether or not the world was going to last long enough for inner conversion to bring about a change in the structure of society seems to have been, if not beyond his interest, possibly beyond his immediate concern. In the meantime, the answer to what such a transformation might have meant or still mean may be less a deduction from what he said than it is an inference from what he did, that is, from the many signs or wonders that he was said to have worked.

Without getting into any technical discussion of just what or what not might be a "miracle" and what different categories of any such thing there might be, let us simply note that according to the gospels not only the followers of Jesus but even his enemies seem to have credited Jesus with certain "startling deeds" to account for his popularity. The same goes as well for a more or less neutral historian writing shortly after that period, Flavius Josephus. Granted that the authenticity of this latter source has been much debated, still, in the eyes of Josephus, who devoted considerably more space to John the Baptist and his death, it was particularly his reputation as wonder-worker that set Jesus apart. That this makes people who may be in search of the historical Jesus uncomfortable is understandable. But that seems to be a problem peculiar to our time, not to people of times past.

Perhaps, as a concession to modern skepticism, we should at least make a broad distinction between the various types of "healings" that Jesus performed and the other wondrous deeds (so-called "nature miracles") that he was said to have done. These first are the kind of thing that is at least thought to be theoretically possible, even today. Inexplicable cures do occur despite the skeptics. Indeed, there are places, such as Lourdes, where skeptics have even been appointed official inspectors with the job or tearing down any possible claims for the supernatural.

If it is conceded that Jesus actually worked or promoted such cures, what was the meaning of his actions? Certainly they were not merely for the sake of philanthropy, despite the frequent mention of Jesus being moved with "compassion". If this had been his only motive, he could have simply healed those who flocked to him and avoided whatever else might cause opposition to him. Nor, again, were these healings for the sake of self-advertisement. Instead, they were meant to be signs of the kingdom already made present. That should be obvious enough, because when Jesus himself was questioned about them, he made it very clear that this is what he was about.

But at the same time, we can hardly speak about this aspect of his ministry or this phenomenon of "signs" or miracles without particular reference to faith. Faith, in the sense of *trust*, seems to have formed a precondition for Jesus being willing to help others. True, there are passages in the gospels where this factor is not explicitly highlighted. And there are other healing stories that instead emphasize faith, or an increased faith, as being the *result* of his activity. Still, there is at least one reference to Jesus not only refusing to heal because of some people's lack of faith but of himself being unable to do so without their faith that they indeed could be healed. Jesus acts like he has no power to heal unless this trusting faith is present. Repeatedly he asks those who besiege him: "Do you have faith?" Or very often, he exclaims: "Your faith has healed you!" Indeed, so much is this trust or "faith" the central ingredient of these stories that we must ask the question from where comes this power of Jesus to heal if not equally from his own faith as well?

This is particularly evidenced in one episode that is described in all three of the synoptic gospels—the healing of an apparently epileptic boy at the request of the boy's father. That this malady, like many others at that time is described in terms of an evil spirit inhabiting the boy should not throw us off track. This was a standard diagnosis of the period. We are even told that some of Jesus' disciples had attempted an exorcism on this boy, but to no avail. Only when Jesus arrives on the scene and gives his command is the boy cured. When asked why it is that he was successful when his disciples were not, Jesus replies that such difficult cases require extra strong faith and just as confident prayer to go with it (some manuscripts add "fasting" as well to Mark 9:29, but this is generally considered a "gloss" or scribal mistake).

That it is not a question of the boy's faith, or even that of the boy's father, who is related to have asked Jesus to strengthen what little faith he had, seems clear enough. The contrast is between the supreme faith in God's power as expressed by Jesus and the apparently hesitant faith of his followers. Jesus may not have said, "You must have faith as strong as my own", but on this occasion he could have hardly made that point any clearer. If the passage in Hebrews 10:2 is the only place in the New Testament where it speaks most explicitly of the faith of Jesus, this account is where it comes a close second.

That Jesus, and not his disciples, possessed the power to bring about such cures presents no problem for those viewing Christ simply as God appearing as a man. He obviously has the power to begin with. But as we can see from a number of other incidents, this view manifestly contradicts the gospel records on several occasions. Even in the "high" christology of the Gospel of John, with its strong emphasis on the divinity of Christ, Jesus is depicted as praying to the Father before he raises Lazarus from the dead (see John 11:41). Although the idea that Jesus was praying aloud for God to grant his wish is proclaimed to be more for the sake of the crowd "that they may believe you have sent me" and "even though I know you always hear me", still, the point is that even here the power of Jesus is seen not as his own, but coming from God.

I stress this approach because if we see this phenomenon from the viewpoint of Jesus' own faith operating cooperatively with the faith of others, the entire matter and problem of miracles makes a whole lot more sense, even to our skeptical modern minds. One of the most disconcerting features of the gospels is the sheer profligacy of these occurrences. This impression is accentuated by the almost uncontested acceptance, even by his most vehement enemies (or, as we have seen, by a neutral historian like Josephus), of the factualness of these cures. So many of them occurred, it seems, that his critics' only weapon was to accuse him of sorcery and diabolic power.

But then, what is to be said as well for the "nature miracles" contained in the gospels, especially those reported by Mark? The calming of the sea, the walking on water, the multiplication of loaves; are not these meant to be taken as miracles or wonders that many were eager to see and report? Yet more often the gospels describe them as "signs" pointing not so much to Jesus himself, but to the kingdom as *already* having arrived, in the midst of this world—at least for those who have "the ears to hear and the eyes to see".

About this latter class of phenomena we can really say little, except point out how much the ancient world took this type of thing for granted and to suggest that perhaps they may, for the most part, be a literary embellishment to highlight the "good news". But here we need to be cautious! True, the ancient world took the frequent occurrence of miracles for granted. But even for them, enough was enough! In a "post-modern" world where the inflexible "laws" of Newtonian physics are rapidly being replaced by what seem to be at most statistical averages of "quanta" existing in a state of fundamental indeterminacy, perhaps we are too quick to write off these reported phenomena as the literary embellishments of the early Christian community. If what we have said about the role of faith in healing is true, particularly a faith that is expressed primarily in the restorative power of love, then who is to say what the limits of the power of faith may be when it comes to some other phenomena as well? Even such a tough-minded biblical scholar like Meier has to admit that at least one of the "nature miracles", that of the mysterious multiplication of loaves and fishes, is so repeatedly referred to in the Gospels that something strange must have actually happened to account for this.

Finally, what about reports of Jesus having raised the dead? Again, probably all we can say about this is that even this sort of thing was ascribed to pagan wonder-workers and for us will probably have to be understood in much the same way as those wonders recounted above.

Faith, Belief and Love

"Love", or really the *confidence* induced by love, could be seen as another name for "faith", at least in the basic gospel sense of the word. But on the other hand, if we focus on what might be called the specifically intellectual content of this faith, the "beliefs" that Jesus affirmed and taught his followers, again we arrive at its close linkage to love. God is a loving Father who welcomes all his children—even us sinners. God's providential love will remove all cause for fear. Our lives are truly in God's benevolent hands. Only those who resist this all-embracing, all-forgiving love need fear.

Again, to attempt to summarize the teaching of Jesus during this period, its underpinning can only be described as faith, even if its most pervasive expression is *love*, the love that forgives enemies, and, again, out of love, would share the goods of this earth with compassion for all. Such love overrides all demands of the Law, indeed, is the sum of all law. It is founded on faith, on the trusting belief that an overriding concern for God's kingdom will both free us from any other concern and at the same time bring all else that we may need besides. Faith in this sense is almost indistinguishable from love. One expresses the other, and *vice versa*. They cannot be separated. "Not everyone who says to me 'Lord, Lord' will enter the kingdom of heaven, but only the one who does the will of my Father in heaven" (Matthew 7:21).

But what exactly is the Father's will? Where is it to be found? The later controversy that we see reflected in the Epistle of James, the problem of belief without expression in love, begins to rear its head here. But we cannot allow it to detain us for long. Suffice to say that we find differing emphases or interpretations in the New Testament depending on the audience and context. The famous passage in Matthew 5:17-20: "I have not come to destroy [the Law or the Prophets] but to fulfill..." etc., as well as a parallel passage in Luke 16:17, has been the subject of much debate. Matthew shows a definite pro-law bias compared to the other gospels. This is readily explainable if his principal audience consisted of Palestinian Christians of Jewish ancestry, or even, in its later Greek rendition, Jews of the *diaspora*. (For a detailed summary of the scholarly discussion of the attitudes contained or combined in the Gospel of Matthew, see Raymond E. Brown and John P. Meier, *Antioch and Rome*, especially Meier's third chapter.)

A similar contrast exists between the Epistle of James with its emphasis on the performance of good works as compared to the theme of freedom from the law in St. Paul's epistles, especially in Romans and Galatians, and Paul's emphasis on "grace". Although Jesus may have really said what Matthew's gospel reports in support of the law, his own actions seem to have been anything but legalistic. So obviously we are dealing with theological interpretation by way of emphasis. But other factors enter into it as well.

Central to such discussions must be recognition of the varying faith stages of the audiences. It is a mark of conventional faith or religiosity to see moral or ethical standards in terms of codes or rules to be obeyed and as sanctioned by external authority. In contrast, when there is a movement towards a more individuative and personally reflective faith, authority becomes more internalized and moral standards generally become more integrated with the logic of the belief system. I say "generally" with some qualifications. Occasionally a superficially "individuated" faith will incorporate a repressive side that re-enforces reliance on an externalized code to keep not-yet-integrated elements in check. The excessive legalism of the Pharisees probably had something of this element to it—perhaps as a counterbalance to too much freedom in their radical reinterpretation of what had been an over-ritualized temple cult.

Bernard Lee, however, has given us another insight to this passion for "jots and tittles". The pharisaic movement can be seen as replacing temple-centered worship, with all its minutiae as detailed in The Book of Leviticus, with a new approach that translated all this rule-keeping into a new home- and synagogue-based and more heart-centered piety. This lay-led religion, where the scribes and rabbis were generally not officially ordained clergy, actually did, as history shows, keep Judaism alive long after the temple and its priestly-led worship had passed from the scene.

However, if Jesus himself, as David Flusser claims, represents a type of piety that could be characterized as a "phariseeism of love", then we are witnessing a still more radical reinterpretation of the old law. Thus Jesus' apparent disdain for the Pharisees' detailed list of rules (they would later be numbered at six hundred and thirteen!) and his insistence on the two commands of love: "You shall love the Lord your God with all your heart, and all your mind, and all your strength; and you shall love your neighbor as yourself" (See Deuteronomy. 6:5 and Leviticus 11:16). Jesus tells us that these indeed sum up the whole law and the prophets (see Matthew 22:37-39; Mark 12:30-31; Luke 10:27). This is radical, and yet, scripturally-based as well. It is no wonder Jesus incited such enmity and suspicion. No one has ever made religion more simple, and at the same time, more difficult!

All this, of course, inevitably leads to the problem of the rejection of Jesus, not so much by the authorities or even by the population which showed some enthusiasm for him at first, but eventually by a sizable number of his would-be followers. That something went wrong and produced a crisis at the end of what we now call the "Galilean ministry" seems to be the almost unanimous conclusion of modern New Testament scholars. They differ only in how much emphasis they give to the change and how they explain it. We will return to this puzzle shortly. But I think that one thing is clear already: neither the religious-political authorities, most of whom were Sadducees, nor the popular religious authorities, who were for the most part rabbis and scribes leaning toward the pharisaic outlook, were ready or able to appreciate the "law of love" approach to human conduct that Jesus preached. They had simply, for the most part, despite all their zeal for the law, or in the case of the Pharisees, mostly because of it, been unable to see through the law to its central foundation in God's love. Or even if they did in an intellectual way, they were nonetheless unable to translate this insight into a love that both sums up and transcends the law beyond a love of the law for its own sake.

For such a mentality, the freedom of the Gospel is a scandal and presents a threat that must be, one way or another, defused of its explosive potential for radical change. This higher law simply remains incomprehensible to those whose faith demands above all the security of knowing they are always right. It has remained a stumbling block not just to the Jews of old, but just as much, or even more, numerically speaking, to many calling themselves "Christians" today. To let go and allow "God to be God" in our lives is equally difficult for all, and theologians and religious bureaucrats can usually be counted on to so qualify any such breakthrough as to render it harmless to the established order.

But still, this does not explain why many of his most devoted followers, who had, by dint of repetition, presumably absorbed this lesson, eventually turned against him. Was it simply, as so many have suggested, that his idea of the kingdom was too heavenly for them? Or was it simply that he failed to live up to popular expectations, fueled by the Zealots, of a royal Messiah, a princely liberator, who at last would "restore the kingdom to Israel"?

Before we consider any other possible cause for the rejection of Jesus, I think that we must first consider this other possibility; that his faith was simply too advanced to be understood or imitated by the rest. What seemed to the Pharisees to be his outrageous behavior maybe confirmed the suspicions of many. That he often ate and drank with sinners, even with tax collectors and prostitutes, may have been refreshing good news, especially to many people. But that this openness must eventually lead, sometimes even to his own amazement, to the conclusion that pagans might even be accepted by God before the Jew—this required an altogether new type of faith.

The Turning Point: The Emergence of Conjunctive Faith

It is hard not to see where Jesus' own preaching and conduct were leading him. He had decided, back in the desert, against popular political zealotry, but people were trying to push him more and more in that direction. He was sent instead to preach a kingdom where the sinners and the outcast were welcomed to join with the "children of God", but official religion would have none of it. John the Baptist, in the meantime, had, quite literally, lost his own head in his confrontation with the corruption of the system. Had Jesus already planned his own little confrontation with the temple authorities? Or was he planning a repeat performance of one enacted earlier? If so, now he had better really think twice! Even some of Jesus' own disciples lost patience with him and began to think, as his relatives had already concluded, that he was deluded or demented. So Jesus left his own country, for the first and only time in his life.

According to the synoptic gospels, Jesus took the twelve with him to the region around Tyre and Sidon on the seacoast of modern Lebanon and from there he traveled back down southeast towards Mt. Hermon and the sources of the Jordan around Dan, which had by then become known as "Paneas", a celebrated pagan shrine. We are often told in older "Life of Christ" type of books that this trip was in the nature of a training mission to make the apostles ready for when he would be gone and they would have to go out on their own and preach the Gospel. Perhaps so, but I doubt that it was intentionally so on Jesus' part. Indeed the first notable incident in this journey had to do with his refusal to cure an epileptic pagan girl because, as he said, he was sent "only to the children of Israel." But the girl's mother importuned, "even dogs under the table eat the children's scraps" (Mark 7:28; Matthew 15:27). She had him there, so he relented and cured the girl, much as he already had cured the centurion's servant at Capharnaum. Again he began to marvel at a pagan's faith.

What we see here, I believe, is the emergence of a new stage of consciousness in Jesus. These repeated incidents where so-called "pagans" displayed more openness and trust than his own people, surely caused a significant change in Jesus' own awareness of his power to reach out to people with the message of God's love. On the one hand, not only the religious establishment, but also even his own people had, for the most part, rejected him. But on the other hand, he saw in these *goyim* or "gentiles" a faith in the sense of a trust and openness to the possibility of God's kingdom that was largely untouched by dreams and expectations of a political messiah.

This was not entirely a new revelation. Recall the long account in the fourth chapter of John's gospel about the encounter with the woman at the well at Shechem. Kurt Aland situates this as being shortly after the death of John the Baptist. If so, after this loss, Jesus must have been even more conscious of the potential "harvest" being great but the "laborers" all too few. That the Samaritans, with their mixed Jewish-pagan ancestry and their rival temple on Mt. Gerizim, were considered worse than mere pagans made little difference. Jesus predicts the day when his Father would no longer only be legitimately worshipped in the temple in Jerusalem, or in any such exclusive or disputed settings. Instead, the day will come when God will be worshipped everywhere "in spirit and in truth" (John 4:23).

But now the situation was somewhat different. If on that earlier occasion Jesus could still boast that "salvation comes from the Jews", it was now becoming apparent that rejection of not only the message of salvation but of the messenger himself also seemed to be coming from his own people. This alone would be enough to make anyone, even a prophet, doubt himself and his mission.

The sudden or even sometimes gradual expansion of awareness that usually is a part of the coming into a truly personal faith is often still limited, and is often tied to a specific location or culture. It typically involves a struggle between self-awareness as an individual as opposed to one's immediate surroundings. At that stage one defines oneself in terms of a role *within* that structure, even while the role itself to a certain extent sets oneself apart from the others. This is the natural setting for the emergence of a "vocation" in the usual sense of the word.

But when one has lived long enough or has been exposed to a wider world, a whole new stage of awareness can emerge. The narrowness of the boundaries within which one's self-awareness and its vocational expression were conceived begins to fall apart. A broader, and sometimes confusing, vision of the world emerges. As the "horizon of consciousness" expands, a new stage of self-questioning very often begins, one that heralds the beginning of a more conjunctive faith. It is "a faith that calls for the integration of elements in ourselves, our society, and in our experience of ultimate reality that have the character of apparent contradictions, polarities, or at least paradoxical elements." (Fowler, 1984. p.64)

"At least"—to put it mildly! The paradox, the contradiction, which is central to the mystery of Jesus and his mission, is revealed in two pivotal incidents in the gospels that form, as it were, a question and an answer. Jesus put the question to his apostles, but the full answer could come only from God.

The Question at Dan

If there were a few more incidents like that on the trip up into Lebanon, we have not been told anything about them. The only other thing we know about this one and only trip that Jesus ever made out of his own country took place near the source of the Jordan River, close to the town of Caesarea Phillipi and the ancient shrine of Dan. It was there, we are told, that Jesus confronted the twelve with the question, "Who do men say that the Son of Man is?" So now he had to ask them, those from whom he hoped for undying loyalty, who they really perceived him to be. It was not an easy question. After beating around the bush a bit, Peter spoke, presumably for the rest. Jesus was the "Messiah" to which Luke adds "of God" and Matthew adds, "the Son of the living God".

Again, what these titles in turn might imply seems to have been the nub of the problem. The synoptic gospels where this incident is recorded, with the exception of Matthew's digression on Peter's future mission, move directly to one common theme; that to be the Messiah means rejection, suffering, and eventually death, yet only to be raised again "on the third day". (Compare Matthew 16:13-20, Mark 8:27-30, and Luke 9:18-21.)

Although all three synoptic gospels include this warning, whether Jesus really did predict his own death and resurrection at this point is a matter of keen debate. Many modern commentators see these "predictions" as a product of editorial hindsight or what the Vatican biblical commission might classify as the second level of tradition—the *kerygma* or a proclamation of post-resurrection faith. On the other hand, it should be pointed out that, following the collapse of his popularity in Galilee, it took no great powers of prognostication to see where the course of his mission was leading him. Too many of the prophets had met a violent death for Jesus to harbor any illusions. But it would only be natural that his most devoted followers would resist this logic.

As for his own resurrection "on the third day", here we may have something else other than the logic of history. If there is any issue on which Jesus clearly stood on the side of the Pharisees, it was this one. Jesus was later not only to declare his firm belief in the resurrection of the dead but gave his own argument, which is an interpretation of Exodus 3:6.

> About the dead rising again, have you never read in the book of Moses, in the passage about the bush, what God said to him: "I am the God of Abraham, the God of Isaac, and the God of Jacob"? He is God, not of the dead but of the living.
> (See Mark 12:18-27.)

That this passage necessarily implies a bodily resurrection, of course, remains debatable. But in the context of a strictly Hebrew view of human nature, which recognized no such thing "soul", at least in the platonic sense of the word (that is, as an immortal spiritual "substance" that can exist entirely independently of the body) the idea of resurrection is the only logically consistent way of expressing belief in eternal life. This is because for a Jew remaining within the confines of a Hebrew vocabulary, only God's breath or spirit (God's *ruah*) could give life to the flesh (the *bashar*) so that one becomes a *nephesh* or "living being". Although for most Jews this *nephesh* might have a shadowy existence of some sort after death in *sheol* or "the Pit" or at best, was somehow gathered into "the bosom of Abraham", only a literal resurrection or reconstitution of the body, much as depicted in Ezekiel's famous vision of the dry bones taking on flesh again and coming back to life, could qualify as true eternal life.

We do not know whether Jesus understood eternal life in such literal terms, but it is probable that the Sadduccees and other Jews coming more under a Greek influence, even had they believed in some form of eternal life, would not have believed in it in precisely these terms. Nor is this to say that for Jesus, as for the Pharisees, a passage like that is quoted above, argued for resurrection to bodily life in exactly the same manner as life lived before death. Previous to this same passage, Jesus attempts to refute the Sadduccees over the question of the status of marriage in the next life, comparing the state of the risen to that of "angels" who "neither marry or are given in marriage." Unfortunately, this response would have meant little to the Sadduccees, who didn't believe in angels either, hence Jesus' final appeal to "the God of the Living, not the dead". (See also Matthew 22:23-33 and Luke 20:27-40). But there can be no doubt that for Jesus the promise of resurrection, for *all* the "just" (that is, the "saved") was very real.

Still, we must ask about Jesus' belief, not in a general resurrection at the end of time or at the coming of the Messiah, but in his *own,* almost immediate, resurrection from the dead. Beginning with the exchange at Dan, we keep running into the phrase "on the third day" (Matthew 16:21 and Luke 9:22) or "after three days" (Mark 8:31). How could Jesus be so sure? It is this phrase, repeated in nearly all the early Christian creeds, that leads many to conclude that this whole resurrection prediction is indeed inspired hindsight, inserted into the gospel accounts long after the event took place. But need it be simply that?

Granted Jesus' strong personal belief in the resurrection, and his twice repeated (according to Matthew: see 12:38-43 and 16:4) comparison of himself to the fabled prophet Jonah, the three-day phrase comes naturally to mind. Despite the fact that from Friday afternoon before sundown to early Sunday morning is, according to Hebrew reckoning, the "on the third day", it is not strictly speaking, as Mark has it, "after three days". Still the comparison still remains apt, if even in a loose way. So too, if Jonah, even by Jesus' own recalling of the story, was "in the belly of the whale for three days and three nights", then, as Jesus is pictured as saying on an earlier occasion, "so shall the Son of Man be in the heart of the earth for three days and three nights" (Matthew 12:40). Taken literally, of course, even by the Resurrection faith-accounts, this was not to be. From these discrepancies we have an additional reason to suspect second-level post-resurrection interpretation, on the one hand, yet, on the other hand, a perfectly logical explanation of why Jesus, if he did strongly believe in his own resurrection, would speak of it as occurring "on the third day".

I raise this whole question in such detail to underline the problem of trying to guess exactly what was in Jesus' mind at any given point. Yet at the same time, it demonstrates why we should not think that this prediction, if indeed it was made on this occasion, was necessarily based on a supposed divine foreknowledge of all that would occur. If Jesus did really make these predictions of his resurrection, it is readily explainable in terms of his beliefs, just as much as the impending sense of his own death seemed already written in the books.

In any case, where other predictions of this sort are recorded, (see Matthew 17:21-22; 20:17-19; Mark 9:29-31; 10:32-34; Luke 9:44b-45; 18:31-34) we are also repeatedly told, especially by Luke, that his disciples could not comprehend what he was saying. So it is unlikely that on this occasion this prediction would have made any more sense. Instead, the evangelists seem to have used this recollection as an opening for a moral lesson about the place of suffering in life, particularly the futility of trying to preserve one's own life, or one's sense of self, in the face of the universal demand that we die to one's self before we can ever expect to truly live.

This same lesson is repeated again on another occasion, in the midst of Luke's rendition of the apocalyptic prediction of the impending disaster awaiting Jerusalem (Luke 17:33). Here we are also cautioned to remember stories of Noah and of Sodom and Gomorrah, and especially the fate of Lot's wife (see Genesis, chapters 8-9 and 19). The emphasis here is obviously on the unpredictable suddenness of the end—whether it is the Romans' destruction of Jerusalem, the end of the world, or simply the end of our individual life. Certainly there is a lesson here for all occasions, but is it simply a warning to "be prepared"?

Here the older *New American Bible* translation (the version before the 1986 revision of the New Testament) of a similar saying in Matthew 10:39 with its rather existential twist ("…he who brings himself to nought for me discovers who he is") delivers a very salutary as well as jarring thought. Surely here we are dealing with something more than just the immediate possibility of martyrdom. Instead we are facing what is the essential paradox of faith—the *risk* that must characterize all religious commitment despite any promise of reward or fulfillment.

With this broader application of this fundamental paradox in mind, perhaps we should also transpose this same understanding back to Luke's version of the exchange that follows Jesus' prediction at Dan. If the parallel Greek texts are not identical, certainly the next verse, especially when the Greek word *psyche* is translated more in keeping with the Hebrew concept of the *nephesh*, also bears this existentialist weight: "What benefit is it to anyone to win the whole world but to forfeit or lose his very self?" (See Luke 9:25 in *The New Jerusalem Bible*; emphasis mine.)

Surely this is one of the most difficult challenges of any religion, indeed of all life. But why is it here, as a kind of meditation, in the midst of what is otherwise a question demanding a straight answer? Perhaps it is because Jesus was asking the same question of himself: who am I really, and what am I accomplishing except to go more inevitably to my death? So die he must, "... but I say to you truly, there are some of those standing here who will not taste death until they have seen the Kingdom of God" (Luke 9:27).

Again, there seems to be some confusion about the exact wording of this last prediction. For Mark it is to be "the kingdom of God in power". For Matthew it is a prophecy of "the Son of Man coming in his kingdom"—an interesting couplet with the earlier Matthean "You are the Christ, the Son of the Living God".

It appears that here, at least, we are dealing with convictions of faith, which is to say beliefs, these read into an earlier situation that demanded a more basic faith or trust that could not see the outcome. Although one cannot simplistically reduce these parallel statements to their common denominator and thereby declare that one has automatically arrived at the actual words of Jesus on this or that particular occasion, it is clear from this sequence of passages, if treated at their face value, that the turning point had indeed come. Any hopes that Jesus or his followers might have had that the kingdom could be inaugurated without bloodshed, without their own martyrdom, were rapidly diminishing. The end time was, at least for them, rapidly approaching and only faith in the coming kingdom of God would see them through.

What I see in all this, if not exactly a "mid-life" crisis, is a mid-career or mid-mission one. The self-questioning that I detect in Jesus' questions about his identity to his disciples parallel, in a way, the same question he was faced to ponder alone in the desert following his baptism. And these, in turn, are foreshadowed by the picture that Luke gave us of the boy Jesus in the temple, who, in questioning the rabbis and scholars, was perhaps somehow groping toward his own self-identity in terms of the "Father" whose "business" he must pursue.

The various crises in the life of faith, as well as those of life in general, are perhaps drawn out too neatly by the developmental psychologists. In particular, although the idea that both adolescence and mid-life are especially times of religious crisis may be true enough, it is more likely that what occurs as such times is more of a beginning of a slow change, rather than anything leading toward a quick resolution. If what I have tried to read into the boyhood temple incident given by Luke marks the beginning of the movement toward a personal faith, what we witness at the Jordan and during the solitary struggle in the Judean desert are milestones on that same critical movement of faith.

So too, what we see taking place during Jesus' reaction to the apparent failure of his Galilean mission and the self-questioning it provokes, although it may mark the sudden onset of a faith that is being forced to become more inclusive or conjunctive in its scope, is not to be quickly resolved! So I hesitate to pinpoint the episode we have just discussed as being indicative of Jesus having suddenly arrived at the stage beyond a purely personal faith or one that is "individuative" even in the broad sense of that term. But the whole situation demands a faith that is more fully integrated or inclusive. The experience of his rejection by his own compatriots, and his growing awareness, however limited, of the trust and openness of many gentiles in his presence, must have caused Jesus to wonder and to ponder about himself and his mission. The resolution of this question, even in part, will determine the whole future of his ministry—what little future was left!

To state my point again, the question "Who do people say that I am?" may reflect Jesus' own questioning of himself and of God's will for him as much as any question the apostles had asked or were perhaps afraid to ask. The answer given to that question, not by Jesus, but by the apostles, is that Jesus truly is the Messiah. But Jesus' own answer to that revelation poses another question, the answer to which the apostles are far from being able to accept. The meaning of that answer, as we have seen, is in the riddle of a suffering and dying Messiah whose cross, in the words of St. Paul, was to be a "folly to the Greeks and a scandal to the Jews" (I Corinthians 1:23).

Yet this is not the whole answer. Like the secret of his true identity, that according to Matthew was revealed to Peter by the Father, the full disclosure of Jesus as the Christ was to be revealed by an experience granted only to Jesus and his closest intimates among the chosen band.

Chapter 4

Toward Jerusalem

The sojourn of Jesus in Lebanon with his closest disciples marked the end of his Galilean ministry. The incident at Dan, with its apparent element of self-questioning, was not completely answered by Peter's "confession"—indeed if that particular declaration of faith took place at that occasion. Or even if it did, it is clear from the rest of the conversation that the apostles still did not understand the full implications of Jesus' messiahship.

The event to which we now turn is even more problematic. Historically speaking, it is impossible to verify. As we shall see, some believe that it represents a post-resurrection experience of the apostles that has been transposed to this location in the synoptic gospels. Yet, psychologically speaking, the timing is perfect. If the sojourn in Lebanon represents the reaction to defeat, and the question at Dan represents the articulation of the crisis, the "transfiguration experience", whatever else may be said about its reality, represents the definitive resolution of the conflict within the mind of Jesus.

The Answer on Mt. Tabor

The "Transfiguration" as it is called, like the Baptism-Temptation story, and like the questioning of the apostles at Dan, to which it is closely connected, forms one of the pivotal points of all three synoptic gospels. In fact, it is in more than one way central to the whole narrative.

According to Matthew and Mark, "after six days" (Luke says "about eight") after the previous incident, Jesus took Peter, James and John with him up a high mountain to pray. There is no certainty that the site of this experience was Mt. Tabor in southeastern Galilee. Some commentators suggest that Mt. Hermon, directly to the east of Dan, might be more probable, even with its high slopes covered with snow much of the year. But wherever the experience may have taken place, we are told that there Jesus was transformed before their eyes. According to Matthew (17:2) "his face shown like the sun and his clothes became a white as the light." Then "suddenly Moses and Elijah appeared to them; they were talking with him" (Matthew 17:2-3). The conversation was, according to Luke (9:31), "of his passing which he was to accomplish in Jerusalem." And just as suddenly, after Peter blurted out his own impulsive reaction, "a cloud came and covered them with its shadow ... and a voice came from the cloud saying 'This is my Son, the Beloved: Listen to him'." (See Mark 9:6 and Luke 9:34-35. The reader is also urged to compare this with Matthew 17:5-18, where the additional phrase appears, "in whom I am well pleased". In addition, in one ancient Syrian version of Luke there appears, instead of "Beloved", the "Chosen One" of Isaiah 42:1.)

Just as suddenly the whole episode is over. On the way down the mountain Jesus explains to them that not only had Elijah returned in the person of John the Baptist and had found only rejection, so too that "the Son of Man will suffer similarly at their hands" (Matthew 17:12). Then he cautioned them to be silent about the whole affair.

What are we to make of this event? Many modern commentators act as if the whole thing never took place. Even such a theological moderate as Walter Kasper (*Jesus the Christ*, 1976) refers to the Transfiguration narrative as simply a "pericope"—a literary unit involving a story and message—without giving any opinion as to its historicity. Others, like Norman Perrin (*The New Testament: An Introduction*, 1974), see it as a transposition of a post-resurrection experience, placed here, at the end of the Galilean ministry, for symbolic reasons. As such it would represent the answer to the problem posed by the Matthean injunction (28:10) that the disciples must journey to Galilee to encounter the risen Christ, something that fails to harmonize with the rest of the synoptic post-resurrection appearances.

On the other hand, John L. McKenzie, writing in the 1968 *Jerome Biblical Commentary* (43:118-119), held that a central mystical experience, equal to importance to the baptismal revelation to Jesus, did occur, but that its reference is not so much to the Resurrection and *Parousia* (Second Coming), as found in Matthew, but, as in the Lukan rendition, to his "passing" (*exodon*) which was to be accomplished in Jerusalem". At the same time the visionary appearances of Moses and Elijah identify Jesus as being the present fulfillment of the Law, as represented by Moses, and the prophets, represented by Elijah. Jesus is seen as bringing to an end that past era, with the Greek word *pleroun* generally translated here as "to be accomplished", literally meaning "to be fulfilled" or "complete". Even Peter's apparent gibberish about "building three "booths" or "tabernacles" has its own Old Testament overtones, since the Jewish feast of Tabernacles—originally a harvest feast—had by then become understood primarily as a commemoration of the giving of the Law on Mt. Sinai.

Clearly whatever the historical basis may have been for this whole episode, its message is central to the unfolding drama of God's plan. It is only through the passion of Jesus, understood as a "passover"—or more exactly, a "passing through" death—that redemption will be accomplished. Despite such an experience being to some degree, like the Resurrection, "metahistorical" in content and mode, or at least interpreted by the evangelists retrospectively in the light of that event, this still does not automatically exclude the possible, or even probable, occurrence of such an experience in the life of Jesus precisely at this time. Instead, it is hard to explain his determination to go to Jerusalem to almost certain death except in the light of such an experience. However, if the apostles' faith and determination were to be similarly strengthened by sharing this revelation, as has been sometimes supposed, it seems hardly born out by their behavior at the time of Jesus' arrest, trial, and execution. This in turn indicates that not only was their understanding of the episode post-resurrectional, but possibly, as a mystical experience, even their full sharing of its meaning was possible only long after the event.

It is in the light of this determination of Jesus to go ahead with his mission—cost him what it might—that I must hazard the guess that for him this occurrence contained the final answer to the great problem posed by his baptismal experience and which was only partially answered by his retreat into the desert. If the Old Syriac variant of Luke that uses the Isaian phrase "my chosen one", which begins the first of the five "Suffering Servant" songs in Isaiah (42:1) instead of "my beloved" as in the other versions of Luke, is any indication, then it was precisely in the role of God's "suffering servant" that Jesus was able to understand the mounting tragedy of his life and mission. In any case, it is here that the synoptic gospels represent Jesus as putting it all together. His messiahship and his rejection are two sides of the same coin. To be called "Son of God", as he is in Matthew's version of the Peter's confession at Dan, may seem to contradict, but it in no way avoids the paradox tied up in his role as the mysterious "Son of Man".

Whether Jesus used this latter title of himself is still widely debated. Some who believe that he did use it also hold that he attached no particular significance to it other than to emphasize his common humanity. But would that in turn not seem to imply that he was conscious of something else? On the contrary, I believe it makes more sense to see this title as derived from the mysterious apocalyptic figure in Daniel, and whether used by Jesus or not, was eventually recognized to be fulfilled in him.

To me it is obvious that the insight provided by the transfiguration experience was a mystical confirmation of what was becoming increasingly evident by any practical assessment of the situation. The Messiah of popular expectation (the "royal" Messiah/"Son of God"), the mysterious apocalyptic

"Son of Man" figure of the last days and the Isaian "Suffering Servant" were both one and the same who Jesus now knew himself to be.

There is a curious parallel to this same paradox found in some of the Essene literature. There we find described a messiah-like "Teacher of Righteousness" who is to meet a martyr's fate, only to be vindicated shortly after by a victorious royal Messiah. Of course, this contrast in roles could be seen in the missions of John the Baptist and Jesus—except that Jesus himself meets the same bloody fate. Jesus hardly meets the expectations of a conquering messiah-king, except in the post-resurrection elaborations of Christian teachings.

Moving back into the realm of Jesus' own consciousness, I believe that what we have here, in terms Jungian analysis, is true "individuation" in the fullest sense of the word, one which is more fully integrative or "conjunctive" in the Fowlerian terminology of our faith development scheme. As I see it, the difference in Jesus' self-awareness after this event is striking—which also explains my uneasiness with Fowler's use of the term "individuative-reflective" instead of merely "personal" as contrasted to a merely "conventional" faith. True, the mission and the self-understanding of Jesus from the time of his baptism was truly and highly individualized in its contrast with Jewish piety in general and to the pharisaic movement as generally understood. Jesus was clearly "his own man" as much as he was God's spokesman. He taught on his own authority, unlike the prophets and teachers who invoked God's name. In this he was different from the rest of God's spokesmen and he knew it. And he made no apologies for it.

Yet the picture was still incomplete, even for him. If we are to take him at his word, he could not say for sure when the end-time, the visible coming of the Kingdom, would occur. It would be soon, he said, the signs of its consummation would begin even during the lifetime of some of his hearers, yet no one, "not even the Son of Man" could know for sure when it would begin (Mark 13:32; Matthew 24:36). And note that this ambiguity is attributed to him *after* the revelation on the mountain, even *during* the last week of his life! If anything, Jesus seems less sure than ever about God's plans for the future, except for one thing—his own suffering and dying.

What I believe we are seeing, at this phase in Jesus' short career, is the beginning of the end, but at the same time, the beginning of his final integration as a person and even of his role as the Christ. Jung tells us that it is the characteristic of the last half of one's life to come to better terms with one's "shadow", one's neglected or even repressed side. Perhaps Jesus had already done this in his desert retreat and that this was what marks his style, especially his compassion for sinners, for the downtrodden, and for women, as so different from the stern baptizer. But he still had to come to terms with his own fate, and this is what I see signified in the accounts of the question to the apostles at Dan and the revelation on the mountain. It is not for mere dramatic effect that each of these events is followed by a prediction of the passion and death. In many ways, the questioning and the vision are only prefaces to the predictions themselves.

The full individuation of Jesus' own faith in his Father could only come about through an integration of what God had in store for him together with what he had already hoped to accomplish for God. What had begun in Galilee in a whirlwind of activity, sometimes so intense that he and his disciples had scarcely time to eat or sleep, now was to be completed by a firestorm of suffering, by a enduring of the taunts and insults, the scorn of indifference, accusations of bad faith, the machinations of authorities, and even betrayal by his disciples. But even these were only words, attitudes and plots. He knew that these would take some time to have their full effect. There was still time to carry on the mission. Not much time, but some. And there still were many people still eager to hear the good news, especially in and around Jerusalem, among both natives of the city and visitors from other parts. Despite the danger of a premature closure of his already threatened mission, he knew he would have to take the risk of conveying his message right into the heart of the capital.

The Power of Vision

It would seem appropriate at this moment to probe a bit deeper, if we can, into the extraordinary power or influence that such a vision or similar phenomenon can have on a person's life.

Abraham Maslow is justly famous for his emphasis on what he called "peak experiences" and their potential to transform one's consciousness, even though, later in his career, he also began to investigate more fully what, in contrast, he called a "plateau experience" or really, *state* of consciousness.

The former "peaks" are seen as momentary, even interruptive episodes that may occur as rarely as once or twice in a lifetime, although there are some who would claim to have them much more often than that. A "plateau" on the other hand, suggests a more or less steady state of peace and deepened awareness, usually the result of long and arduous discipline involving asceticism, concentrated prayer and meditation. However, I suspect that the two phenomena can coexist, with someone who lives on a plateau on occasion transported beyond what has become his or her normal state of awareness. This is what I would envision to be the case with

Jesus—the transfiguration being the most outstanding and remarkable incidence of this state attributed to him.

Despite the popularity of Maslow's original term, we are not talking here about mere moments of bliss, whether they are a deepened sense of the beauty of the world or another person, or a vague but comforting sense of oneness with all reality. What has been pictured in this episode is an extraordinary rapture, one so astounding that the details, as witnessed by the three specially chosen apostles, Peter, James and John, are repeated in all three of the synoptic gospels with only the slightest variations and is mentioned yet again, in the much later Second Epistle of Peter—the authorship of which has been much disputed, yet which may be even more a sure indication of a major tradition. Yet, as in so many other central points, it is again strangely missing in John, the most "mystical" of the gospels. Still, there can be no question of the significance that the New Testament places upon this episode.

Many would deny the objectivity of the experience, or would locate it entirely within the imagination of the three "witnesses" who would also remain suspect because of their near total agreement on what they each "saw". On the other hand, there are those who credit Jesus with a plateau-like sense of constant divine self-awareness, and would conclude that the phenomenon, if it occurred at all, only took place for the sake of the apostles and would have left Jesus psychologically unmoved. Contrary to the totally skeptical as well as pious "docetists"—those who continue to see Jesus' humanity as merely a holy show put on for our sake—it is hard to explain the importance the New Testament places on this episode unless something happened that affected Jesus himself as well.

No doubt the apostles were greatly impressed by something. But just *what* it was, that is, what they actually saw with their eyes, as against what they may have imagined in their minds, whether individually or collectively, or even *when* the meaning of the experience impressed itself upon them; all this is open to question.

However, I think we miss the point entirely if we fail to see this as an experience primarily *of Jesus* as well. I say this, again, because psychologically it all fits. This episode was born out of a time of crisis, a point where not only the question—"Who do you say I am?" and the self-doubt it portrays—but even the answer as well ("You are the Messiah", including the Matthean addition, "the Son of the Living God") are forebodings of a coming disaster. They point to a kind of martyrdom that goes far beyond the possibility or even certainty of death. They also point to a coming test of faith that cannot ever be fully resolved until it is too late to reverse the process already set in motion.

This new test of faith is, in a way, even more difficult than a simple but painful matter of accepting one's fate. In the light of such a vision or experience, faith, in at least one sense, disappears. Those who undergo such a thing can be said to no longer "believe", but instead truly *know* (or think they now know) what before they only "believed". Their convictions, which up to this time may have been merely "projected analogies"—suppositions made about God on the strength of ideas and feelings taken from others, from parents, from other authority figures, or other influences—are replaced by first-hand experience of the transcendent. They no longer "believe" that God exists. They have "seen" God or have been "touched by God" directly. And more often than not, what they have experienced is, and remains, indescribable.

One would think that to have reached such a pass would be entirely enviable. But to the contrary, this is where a new kind of martyrdom begins, that is, if one has the strength to act on the basis of such an experience. "Martyrdom" in the original sense of the Greek word *martyros* means to "witness" to speak out or act out in testimony to what one believes or knows to be true. That many or most such martyrs end up being killed for their convictions is a secondary, though hardly minor, detail. Alive or dead, a martyr must proclaim a faith. But the more significant question is whose faith in whom—in God or in one's own self?

Here we have repeated what is the crucial transition from a merely "conventional" faith to a truly "personal" faith, but this time on a whole new level. In the first transition, one usually exchanges an inherited set of beliefs for a new personally chosen set of beliefs, or else, through a truly personal commitment, makes this given set of beliefs one's own. But the beliefs or convictions, in a sense, are "exterior" to oneself: they have been received from elsewhere, or perhaps acquired from serious study or after long experience with life. The next stage, "conjunctive faith", normally results from a combination of increased experience and study with perhaps, not infrequently, a certain mellowing or wisdom that often, but unfortunately not always, comes with age.

This time, in the wake of such experiences, the personal element reaches a new depth in a whole new, and sometimes frightening, way. My personal faith can no longer be in God as someone else defines, presents or mediates God, or God's image, to me. Instead, once one experiences God directly, no one else's description or image of God can be substituted for my own. At best it can only strengthen my own impression—or else, make me doubt myself and my experience all the more!

In a very real sense, then, the experience of God will either destroy faith as we have known it, or will end up destroying all faith in ourselves as well. For faith can no longer merely worship the image of God given to us from elsewhere, but must be able to incorporate our own experiences of God or else become alienated from our deepest intuitions.

But the possibility of self-alienation goes deeper yet. Faith, taken in its most radical and original gospel sense can no longer be trust in a God who speaks to me from "outside". It must now be a trust in a God who has spoken to me, or touched me in the deepest recesses of my own mind or heart; a God whom I believe has spoken to me from "within".

Even more this means, that not only I no longer have to "believe" in God, but that most of all I have to believe in myself and my own experiences, to believe that my own intuitions are not crazy, that my mind has not slipped its moorings and that I am not adrift on a wild sea of self-delusion. This remains a frightening and very real possibility.

Carl Jung, who of all psychiatrists and psychologists was the most open to mysticism and most insistent that mere belief had to be superseded by direct experience for the human psyche to grow and reach maturity, had no illusions about this. "Religious experience" he wrote "is *extra ecclesiam* (outside the church), subjective, and liable to boundless error!" (C.G.Jung, Psychology and Religion, *Collected Works*, 74:1938.) That Jesus, the most pious of Jews, already found himself regarded as "outside the church", regarded as an anathema by both the Sadduccees as well as the Pharisees, is obvious enough from both the gospels of Luke and of John. Humanly speaking, he was becoming more and more isolated from all but his closest disciples—whose reliability he knew to be questionable at most. It is no wonder that by this point in his life, his faith, more than ever before, had to be a faith in his own unique experience of God.

I am in no way implying that, up to this time, Jesus really had never had a fully in-depth religious experience. Far from it. I have argued all along that his consciousness of God as "Father" spoke eloquently of the extraordinary depth of his personal contact with God. From this point of view, what happened on Mt. Tabor, or wherever or however this experience took place, may only represent another in a long line of such revelatory encounters.

But this time, there was one big difference. Until then he could have still turned back and allowed himself to sink into relative obscurity. He had disappointed the masses in Galilee, but he had not alienated them. He could still have been careful to say nothing upsetting to the authorities and to heal the sick and still speak of the loving Father in heaven who looks after all, and they, in turn, would have let him sink slowly out of sight.

But not after this: God had spoken not only to him but also to his most loyal companions, and even brought in the spirits of Moses and Elijah as witnesses to God's plan. He must, if he is to be obedient, go through with his mission to the end. Now there can be no turning back.

The Mission in Judea

Jesus was no fool. He took his time and apparently planned his moves carefully. John's gospel speaks of an undercover trip to Jerusalem for the fall feast of Tabernacles and again in December for the Feast of the Dedication. All this is hard to fit into the supposed chronology of the synoptics, but still seems quite plausible. For our purposes however, this renewed and broadened period of ministry serves an important purpose. It illustrates that full integration of faith, including the acceptance of the inevitable, still does not mean a premature capitulation of any sort. The approach of night, as Jesus observed, should spur us to greater activity while there is still the light by which to see. Herein is the difference between a prophetic sense of destiny and commitment to action as contrasted to fatalistic cowardice. A mature faith is able to accept death as part of life. A lack of faith is characterized by a rejection of life that would, if it could, rob death of any significance.

I realize that it is questionable in the scholars' eyes to take John's gospel as representing the historical facts with any accuracy. Nevertheless, I still am attracted to Bishop J.A.T. Robinson's claim that this gospel, at least in parts, despite its thematic structuring and theological embellishment, does contain some of the most accurate and detailed information about Jesus' final months of ministry in and around Jerusalem.

We often see the objection that Jesus, as presented in the fourth gospel even sounds different, speaking especially of himself in a way that we rarely if ever find in the synoptic gospels. But the distinction between the three layers of tradition found in the gospels largely solves this difficulty, especially if we think of the famous "I am" sayings as found in John—most particularly those expressing his union with God—as third level material cast into first person speech. It can be occasionally helpful to transpose these first person sayings in John's gospel into the third person instead of trying to locate the point that divides between what we might conceivably imagine Jesus saying and what obviously ends up as a theological discourse in the author's words put into Jesus' mouth. The ancient world was not imperceptive when it called John the Evangelist "the Theologian", even though such literary devices were still in vogue. As we shall soon see, there may be yet another reason for this language. Nevertheless, in the meantime, I am inclined to believe, with Bishop Robinson, that some of the detailed descriptions in the Gospel of John, for example, of places, or some of the customs, are uncannily accurate, or at least enough so that we can gain some interesting insights from these alone.

For example, why did Jesus first decline to travel to Jerusalem (John 7:2-13) and then, after the others had left, go up secretly, when the feast was half over, suddenly make an appearance in the temple, preaching not so much about the kingdom it seems, but according to what is reported in John, about his own authority to teach and this precisely on matters of interpretation of the Law? (See John 7:14-24.) John then presents us with a series of theological discourses and debates with the authorities that Jesus seems unlikely to have expected to get away with, yet he as much as defies them to lay a hand on him (John 7:14 through 10:51). Even the interruption of these discourses by the incident of the adulterous woman (John 8:1-11— a passage judged by some to be from an independent non-Johannine source) and the curing of the man born blind (the whole of Chapter 9) seem to be calculated to provoke the authorities. If so, these incidents seem to have been particularly effective.

However, we should notice that even these actions were not directed against the abuses of the temple and its ritual that so angered Jesus and which provoked him at an earlier date, according to John 2:13-17. If this early passage truly reflects a different occasion than the Palm Sunday "cleansing of the temple", and at the same time is distinct from "the feast of the Jews" (the Passover?) mentioned in John 5:1, then we also must conclude that Jesus was being very bold indeed. If so, the authorities were probably waiting for a repeat performance of that earlier hot-blooded act. It would be hard to convict him on the basis of anything he was saying— particularly if we follow the synoptics as a more accurate record of the style of his speech. No doubt some incident in the temple, where the Jewish authorities, as distinct from the Romans, had almost full jurisdiction, was probably eagerly awaited by those who would harm him. Most likely Jesus' ultra-cautious approach to Jerusalem, despite his apparent last-minute change of mind, was really because of his awareness that real danger awaited him and that he would have to assess the situation carefully, in person, before making his final move.

If all this sounds too calculating and not spontaneous enough to qualify as abandonment to the inspiration of the Spirit, I will have to disagree. God rewards us for courage, not for stupidity. The "simplicity" recommended in the gospels is a straight-forwardness born of single-mindedness or lack of ambivalence. Otherwise it is hard to imagine it in combination with the wisdom or cunning of the serpent. It does not mean setting ourselves up to be a "pigeon". A fully integrated faith can combine both qualities; both trust in God and prudential judgment. Fanaticism is neither the mark of true wisdom or true faith—at least not of a faith that has reached a more mature, "conjunctive" stage. No doubt if Jesus had shown up before and upset the moneychanger's tables and the birdcages, the authorities would have written him off as some provincial fanatic. This time they would not, and Jesus decides to hold his tongue and bide his time. Besides, probably most people saw little harm in this "sacred commerce". It was for the convenience of the worshipers was it not, so why not allow it in the temple? Certainly there were more important issues than that at stake.

Something else is striking about Jesus' words and conduct at that time. Not that it was basically different from before, but there seems to be a deeper awareness, not only of the workings of the Spirit within his own life, but within the lives of others as well. This is brought out especially in the long episode of the cure of the man born blind. Without repeating the whole story (John 9:1-41) it is enough to simply point out one saying of Jesus about divine judgment and punishment that all too often even good people of sincere, but misdirected, faith are apt to overlook. "Who sinned", asked the apostles, "this man or his parents that he should be born blind?" "Neither" replied Jesus: if there was an divine reason, he adds, it was so that God's glory could be demonstrated by this cure—and even here I suspect this is John's added reasoning. Be that or not, Jesus now sounds a bit different from when he threatened divine punishment on Chorozain, Capharnaum, and Bethsaida for their unbelief. Even if God sometimes allows accidents to happen, he does not single out punishments for the guilty in the manner some people would like to imagine. (Compare this with a remark Jesus made on an earlier occasion about the Galileans executed by Pilate, or the victims of a collapsing tower, as reported in Luke 13:2-5.)

We should also note the story told about him and the woman accused of adultery. Although Jesus hardly condones her sin—as some might think from his lack of rebuking her—he sees everyone to be sinful yet forgivable in God's eyes. Again, for the truly integrated personality that is typical of conjunctive faith, the law is written in the heart, and that law is above all one of love. The loving sinner is closer to God than the lukewarm "saint".

Again—although this latter passage seems to have more affinity with Luke's gospel, especially when it comes to the question of Jesus' treatment of women—we are still brought back to the issue of the Johannine discourses and their disconcerting language. I have already alluded to the skepticism these passages elicit from the historical-minded, as well as hinted how I find myself best able to deal with them as theological meditations. But I think that if we treat them entirely in this manner we are in danger of loosing a something of great importance. True, they may represent an objectification of Jesus' inner life with the Father by means of a style of language that is peculiar to the Johannine school. Some would see that this imagery, with its dualistic contrasts of light-darkness, good as opposed to evil, spirit versus flesh and other almost gnostic-sounding phrases derives from the Essene literature of the period. Perhaps that is possible.

At one period in the history of critical scriptural scholarship, before anything was known about the Essenes other than their name, it was thought that the language of John's gospel was too theologically sophisticated to belong to Palestinian sources and had to be ascribed to much later, even third- or fourth-century, Greek Christian writers. Then a fragment of this gospel (now known as the Chester Beatty Papyrus II or "p46") was found in Egypt and carbon dated to the early second-century, turning out to be the oldest surviving piece of New Testament manuscript that we presently have. I mention all this as a warning about jumping to conclusions based on hypotheses that happen to "explain" certain similarities, or, on the other hand, would explain them away. There are even those who have even advanced a theory that John's gospel also shows clear signs of Buddhist inspiration!

The possibility of John, or even Jesus, having been influenced by the Essenes or even more esoteric ideas is not as "far out" as some might think, at least if we begin to think more in terms of conjunctive faith. To rule them out as contaminating the simple, stark purity of the synoptics is perhaps to judge more from a cultural bias than strong evidence, one way or another. The language of the Jesus presented by John is difficult to reconcile with the Jesus of Matthew, Mark, and Luke is obvious enough. But to ignore, on that account, the insights that the Johannine gospel provides could be a tremendous mistake. Not that the "sayings" of Jesus in John are the *ipsissimi verbi*—the actual words of Jesus himself. But they may well be the in-depth interpretations of John the mystical theologian into the hidden mysticism of Jesus himself. Unless we understand them at least on this level, instead of dismissing them as "unhistorical", hence valueless as far as trying to understand the "real" Jesus, we will be in great danger of misunderstanding or missing the significance of Jesus altogether. Only those who have failed to reach a more integrated, "conjunctive" faith could fail to see the deeper, existential realities that lurk beneath the surface of the Johannine narratives.

In a certain sense, Jesus knew himself to be "one" with the Father, existing in the mind of God, the great "I AM"—the name *Yahweh* believed to have been derived from the Hebrew root meaning "to be". Hence the frequency of the "I am" sayings found in John, or phrases like "Before Abraham came to be, I am." (See John 8:31f.) So too, if he already sensed that if he was the Messiah-Son as revealed in the mystical experience on the mountain, then he would also be "lifted up" as the serpent in the desert. But at the same time, must fall into the ground in death to self, much as a single grain of wheat, before his life could bear fruit. The language is strikingly different from the simple aphorisms of the synoptics, no doubt. But for those who read the secrets of his heart, like John, the conclusions will ultimately be the same.

"No man has spoken as this man." This was true of Jesus as the world saw him and heard him at the time. But for those who had those same eyes to penetrate the outer man or the ears to probe the secrets of his speech, a much deeper and more universal truth emerges. It is a truth that permeates all true religions, indeed, even the most fundamental, and the most profound philosophies of life. Indeed, it is only if we let go of our lives that we shall find them again. It is only in dying that we live.

Chapter 5

Passing Over

What is a vocation? A call and a response. This definition does not say everything: to conceive the call of God as an expressed order to carry out a task certainly is not always false, but it is only true after a long interior struggle in which it becomes obvious that no such constraint is apparent. It also happens that the order comes to maturity along with the one who must carry it out and that it becomes in some way this very being, who has now arrived at full maturity. Finally, the process of maturing can be a mysterious way of dying, provided that with death the task begins...there has to be a dizzying choice, a definitive dehiscence [rupture] by which the certitude he has gained of being called is torn asunder. That which—as one says, and the word is used rightly here — consecrates a vocation and raises it to the height of the sacrifice which it becomes is a breaking of the apparent order of being, with its formal full development or its visible efficacy.　　　(Pierre Emmanuel, *La Loi d'exode,*
　　　　　　　　　　　Translation by Thomas Merton)

In some ways, this quotation, which caught the attention of the popular American religious writer (*The Asian Journal of Thomas Merton*, 1968, p.169) shortly before his death, sums up the mystery of the final weeks of Jesus' life. The unitive experience of the Transfiguration, for all its glory, was but the prelude to the Cross. The brief triumph of Palm Sunday was to end in the ignominy of Calvary. The raising of Lazarus from his tomb was to lead to Jesus' own sojourn among the dead.

All this brings us to a further question about the faith of Jesus. Did his faith reach perfection in his short life? To answer this, we have to go back and examine what faith development theory itself says and only then assess the possibilities and the probabilities on the basis of what we read in the gospels.

One of the most controversial areas in the whole topic of faith development, is whether there is really a *unitive* stage beyond the fully individuated and integrated form that James Fowler has termed

"Conjunctive Faith"? And the answer to that question, of course, depends a great deal on whether we are talking about a new, distinctive type of faith or simply a new deepening of what already is there. I believe that it is truly a case of the latter, but that it is not something that a person can bring about on his or her own initiative. Although it may be objected that this is true regarding any growth or stage in faith, this is particularly true of this final stage. It is a transformation of that faith that already exists, but it is a change that is brought about most of all by divine initiative.

That the Transfiguration represents such a transforming unitive experience—at least to the apostles' minds—there can be no doubt. However, here again Maslow's distinction between what is a "peak experience" and a "plateau experience", would be useful. True mystical experience is, almost by definition, unitive. But just as a peak experience does not necessarily lead to a plateau or continuation of the same, neither does a momentary mystical transport, even one specially initiated by God, necessarily result in a constant state of conscious awareness of union with God. But it would be precisely this continuing state of awareness of divine union that I would understand to be "unitive faith".

So the second question that must be faced is whether Jesus himself did arrive at this final stage of faith. Excepting those who see the whole topic of Jesus having to possess faith as non-negotiable, here we have to face the presumption that if he did possess faith, his faith would have been necessarily the greatest that could be possibly imagined. In short, how could we possibly countenance any doubt about the absolute perfection of the faith of Jesus?

Nevertheless, if we are to be consistent in our approach, basing our estimation on the gospel indications of the psychological states of Jesus, as slim as this evidence may be, then no question is out of bounds, even if we have little hope of a satisfactory answer.

Here too we have to face the fact that there are people who, looking at the evidence these slim documents provide, have concluded that Jesus' faith was something less than perfect, at least until just before the very end. Such an opinion, however, must be tempered by the realization that people's judgments are affected by their own cultural and personal values. For example, some would see Jesus' decision—was it an outburst of temper? — to cause a scene in the temple a second time as something not only provocative but downright reprehensible. Likewise, there is the apparent peevishness evidenced during the final week of his life in the strange little story told about him cursing a fig tree for bearing no fruit and this out of fruit-bearing season! (See Mark 11:12-14 and Matthew 21:18-19a.) And of course, Jesus still had his own cultural limitations, remaining a Jew up to the end—even if later writings reverse the impression by giving him an anti-Semitic flavor.

In the last chapter, I suggested that an experience like the Transfiguration can transform faith itself in some striking, even paradoxical ways, but most of all, the transformation takes place in the psychological stance of the believer. Fowler has described the change as a radical "decentration" from self or a state of "egolessness". Normally, such a transformation is effected, according to Western mystical teaching, by a so-called "Dark Night" or "Night of Faith"—to use the terminology adopted from St. John of the Cross. It is generally distinguished from the more active "night of the senses" and from other forms of self-purgation and detachment by its passive nature, in that it is not normally sought but instead inflicted. At the most, one might prepare oneself for this trial, but to actively court it, to force God's hand, would probably be an indication that one is still too egocentric to be an apt subject for this final purification. Instead, the situation takes on the character of an impasse where one, in attempting to carry out the divine will, reaches a point where nothing more can be done other than to deliver oneself up to a total and uncompromising dependence upon God.

Self-Abandonment and Martyrdom

People like to suppose that when such a total transformation or abandonment to God's will takes place that religious fervor somehow carries persons through their trial in a burst of confidence and consolation. We like to think that if faced with such a trial, God's grace would bring us through the ordeal psychologically, as well as spiritually, intact. Indeed, there are enough martyr legends coming from the early days of Christianity, as well as more recent accounts from modern times, that give such an impression. Undoubtedly, some specially graced persons, whether martyrs or mystics, or possibly both at once, seem to pass into such a state without any perceptible sense of spiritual trial. But this is rare, and, I suspect, more apparent than real. More likely they have already passed through this purgation in a less perceptible way—or perhaps the accounts are simply incomplete. It is much more usual that the person in question suffers, for a time, a sense of total abandonment by God.

The indications and implications are clear in the gospel accounts of Jesus' passion and death. Consider the story of the bloody sweat in the Garden of Gethsemane (Luke 22:44) and the depiction by all three synoptics of his prayer to God that he might, if possible, escape the fate that awaited him. These point to a trial of faith that goes much deeper than popular Christian piety, formed by ages of what is often termed "high christology", can allow. Usually, according to these views, his Agony in the Garden had two causes. One would have been his natural physical shrinking from the torments that he knew awaited him—a view that also fits in well with the approach taken by this book. But the other interpretation would have the cause of his agony to have been his divine foreknowledge. According to this view, despite what he was about to go through, he would have already known that his suffering would fail to save all those sinners, from Judas Iscariot on to the end of the world, who would refuse to repent and continue to resist divine grace to their own damnation. And this foreknowledge, in turn, would have made his agony all the worse.

However, even without such divine foreknowledge, we must not deny the enormity of the suffering that merely premonitions such as these would have caused. Undoubtedly Jesus had seen, first hand, Roman treatment of criminals previous to his own arrest, and with such a fate in mind, he would now particularly agonize over the seeming failure and utter futility of his mission. Still, such an analysis of the cause of his suffering seems superficial compared to what I'm inclined to think was really the case. One could suffer such dread and disappointment without one's faith being really tested to its depths. But I think it is clear, from the account of his words on the cross, that he truly suffered such a test of faith.

Eli, Eli, lama sabachthani! ("My God, my God, why have you abandoned me?") How can we explain away such heart-rending words? Centuries of theological debate have not reduced the puzzle or the scandal of this cry. True, they form the opening line of Psalm 22. No doubt, in the evangelists' minds they conjure up the memory of this whole psalm as somehow prophesying the passion and death of Jesus, or even represent an effort to tell us what final prayers were on Jesus' parched lips. But that he was actually abandoned by God, or even thought he was abandoned, seems unthinkable. Elaborate theories were fashioned by medieval theologians to explain how this could be, such as a suspension of his human consciousness of his unity with the Father or a momentary deprivation of his habitual enjoyment of the "beatific vision". But that his sense of faith had reached a nadir—which was paradoxically at the same time the epitome of pure, unalloyed abandonment into the hands of the Father—seemed impossible to imagine, particularly if one rules out the possibility of Jesus having faith in the first place.

Here we also have to face more specifically one question that we have already explored in our earlier consideration of Jesus' predictions of his suffering, death, and resurrection. Particularly, what are we really to think of the statement, "On the third day he will rise"? And again we must face, from the onset, that this prediction, if not these predictions in their entirety, is generally considered by modern scholars to be a retrospective interpolation by the evangelists—a stock creedal formula from the earliest *kerygma*. No doubt this could be possible without destroying our view of the general reliability of the gospels. Such an explanation also makes the incomprehension of the apostles a little more believable, since otherwise the statements that they didn't understand what Jesus was talking about at the time sound just a trifle naive. More likely they simply didn't believe him. Nevertheless, if Jesus made these predictions about his being delivered up and put to death, I think that it makes more sense, psychologically speaking, as well as for the reasons outlined earlier (in Chapter 3), to hold that he also believed he would rise.

My reason for holding this opinion is this: if Jesus had come to the conclusion that the only way his mission could be completed was through his own death, then it is only logical to believe that he, as a believer in the resurrection of the dead, also believed that his mission would be vindicated by his being raised again. If he had come to identify in his own mind, rightly or wrongly, with the Isaian "Suffering Servant" songs, the mysterious "Son of Man" figure in Daniel, and those associated with the somewhat ambiguous popular speculation on his "messiahship", it seems only consistent that he also would grasp at belief in his vindication through resurrection—even should he otherwise fail.

There is an eerie parallel here to the temptations during his desert fast. Then it seemed that two routes that promised pseudo-success were rejected; popular demagogic "messiahship" on the one hand, and political intrigue on the other. Perhaps the first was still possible. The Palm Sunday reception in Jerusalem symbolizes the continuing temptation in this direction. But the second was no longer a viable option. He had become the implacable enemy of the establishment. But a third possibility, to force God's hand in a radical gesture of abandonment to divine providence, was no longer a seemingly suicidal "tempting of God". It was now being demanded of him! If he really believed in God, and really could have been tempted by the belief that "God's angels would bear him up, lest he so much as injure his foot against a stone", how much more must he now face this test of faith sent to him directly as part of his God-given mission as he now understood it? Now it was all or nothing, and he knew it. It was either this or the abandonment of his whole mission—or what was left of it.

But there is another reason for my contention regarding Jesus' own belief in his resurrection. When I speak of the "faith of Jesus" I am not simply speaking of his human trust in God. True, throughout this book I have emphasized an understanding of faith that leans heavily toward a notion of risking oneself in radical trust, this instead of seeking consolation in doctrinal security. But still, one has faith in a specific form, and trust in God is never intellectually content-free. We generally believe that God will do such and such for us and, if God cares for us and if we live our life for God, our life will not have been lived in vain. The apparent failure of Jesus' life-mission would have been, to all appearances, complete—unless it were vindicated by something more than just a tragic memory.

St. Paul saw this clearly, and argued in a context that was not very receptive to the idea of resurrection: "If we will not rise, then neither has Christ risen, and if this is the case, then our faith is in vain" (I Corinthians 15:12-14). So too, in the context of Jesus' own beliefs, there could be no trust in God apart from the hope of his own resurrection. To have denied this would have been the first step toward capitulation to the alternatives he had already clearly rejected—popular or political immortality, such as it exists.

But like that fatalistic temptation in the desert—perhaps repeated more than once along that temple balustrade where his disciple James would be hurled to his death not many years later—death must be the ultimate test of faith. "If you are the Son of God, throw yourself down..." So now, he must let himself be thrown down, to be nailed to a cross-beam and then be "lifted up" not by the wings of angels, but by rough Roman soldiers, to die. As for the "stone", it would be rolled against his tomb, should he be lucky enough to be given one.

No doubt, from an existential point of view, Jesus' decision to deliver himself into the hands of his enemies can be seen only as the ultimate "leap of faith", while his dereliction on the cross—his "Godforsakeness" as the German evangelical theologian, Jürgen Moltmann (*The Crucified God*) terms it—remains as the outward expression of what only could have been the greatest test of faith imaginable. So too his forgiveness of his enemies and his final abandonment into the hands of God, his Father, remain the highest expressions of faith imaginable. Beyond this, little else can be said.

But at this point, if the gospels remain silent—the original closing of the Gospel of Mark simply ending with the startled profession of faith by the centurion as Jesus bows his head in death—Christian faith and theology has refused to do so. Instead, a certain theological mythology took over, one that does not so much jump to the object of Jesus' belief in the resurrection but first explores the meaning of death itself. The self-abandonment of Jesus on the cross, surely, was not the end. But neither could a more reflective Christianity leap to the belief in the Resurrection without first understanding that a passing-over must also be a *passing-through.*

The Descent into Hell

The Decent into Hell, found in the traditional baptismal or "Apostles' Creed" is a long-neglected and widely misunderstood theme of Christian antiquity. Indeed, it seems to have been relegated to the status of a theological curiosity kept artificially alive by the Eastern Church liturgies more than by any doctrinal concern. Just what is the meaning of this strange, mythological-sounding phrase?

For one, it should be made clear that the words, in the Latin version of that particular creed are *"descendit ad inferus"* not *"infernus"* (sic). That second letter "*n*" makes a big difference. The reference here is not to "hell" in the sense of *gehenna* or the place of punishment depicted in the synoptic gospels. It is rather to *sheol,* the grave or "pit" of Old Testament usage. This netherworld of the dead (the realm of *Hades* in the Greek version of this same creed) reflects the ancient Hebrew uncertainty about the fate of the dead. To the Jewish mentality of that time, lacking a clear concept of an immortal soul, the only possible way that a person could survive death would by a reversal of the process of dying. But even here there is no substantive or Hebrew noun for the idea, only the verbal affirmation that the dead, at least those of pious memory, will "rise up [or be raised up] again". Hence eventually there appeared the term "resurrection", or in Greek, *anastasia,* that is "to be standing" (*stasis*) "again" (*ana*).

Obviously, this whole idea was controversial, even in Jesus' time. The biblical first hints of the concept are found, in Ezekiel's (37:1-14) famous vision of the "dry bones" but it is clearly meant as a prophecy of the restoration of the Jewish nation. In the book of Daniel (12:1-4), we find more than what appears to be just a literary device. A clearly doctrinal statement comes only in II Maccabees (7:14), a book not accepted in the present Jewish canon of scriptures—hence termed "deuterocanonical" by Catholics and "apocryphal" by the reformation churches. But inter-testamental Jewish literature gives evidence that the idea was widespread, even if not universally accepted, by Jesus' time.

One point of debate, even among those who accepted the idea, was whether this raising up would be universal—including both the wicked as well as the good—or that instead it only applies to the good. St. Paul's discussion of the matter in his letters to the Corinthians and Thessalonians would seem to favor the latter opinion. Resurrection can come about only through our mystical-sacramental identification with Christ, and even then, it is more of a transmutation into a whole new type of existence instead of any continuation or repetition of the old.

On the other hand, the gospel references to resurrection, especially as found in John 5:29, seem to be a resurrection to either reward or punishment. The wicked will rise to be given their just deserts. Hence Jesus' frequent allusions to *gehenna*, especially in the Gospel of Matthew where it appears seven times. "The Valley of Hinnon" (*Ge Hinnon*) was the city dump of Jerusalem—where the fires burned day and night and plenty of worms were to be found. (This same image is found at the very end of the book of Isaiah the Prophet—it is not some notion of divine vengeance unique to Christianity!)

So what is my point? It is this: Jesus' belief in the resurrection, as firm as it may have been, was bound to have been not only controversial in the first place, but somewhat uncertain in specific content as well. Clearly, like Paul, he did not see it as a continuation of our old earthly state, as can be seen from his sharp rebuttal of the Sadducees who derided the whole idea from the start. According to Jesus, "They [the risen] will be like the angels, neither marrying nor giving in marriage" (Matthew 22:30; Mark 12:25). Yet, on the other hand, he seems to have taken the idea of netherworldly physical torment as a punishment for sin as a distinct possibility. To write off his warnings about *gehenna* as a mere concession to the folk-mentality of his listeners is to take an easy way out of what has become an embarrassment to modern sophistication. On the contrary, it may just as well have been a scandal to his hearers of that time, especially to the more sophisticated Jerusalem crowd, the Sadducees in particular—who didn't believe in angels either.

How could Jesus be so sure of his views? Or was he really all that sure? Perhaps we'll never know. And this is also my point in my excursion into this ancient teaching about the "descent" to the netherworld, to the grave, in death. In his death, Jesus, humanly speaking, was giving himself up totally to the unknown. He was experiencing in himself totally, existentially, that terror which death inspires. Faith—in the sense of belief —is a kind of knowledge, but it is a knowledge that is sure only to the extent that it is prepared to give itself over entirely to uncertainty in trust. As the mystical theologian, John of the Cross, wrote in *The Ascent of Mt. Carmel*:

To come to the knowledge you have not,
You must go by a way you know not. (Book I, Chap. 13.11)

The same might be said, just as truly about the ascent of Calvary and the descent into the grave.

Early Christian, especially Greek and Oriental Christian theology, elaborated this "descent" theme in various ways. One takes the form of a mythic triumphal procession, as it were, through the Gates of *Hades* or, more optimistically, to the "Paradise of the Fathers", roughly equivalent to the Jewish concept of "Abraham's Bosom", to lead all the saints of the Old Testament to New Testament glory. Another theme, frequently depicted in the standard Resurrection icons of the Eastern Churches, is Christ, holding his cross, now as a scepter or standard of glory, leaning over to give his hand to help Adam and Eve emerge from their graves. All this is, of course, a highly symbolic depiction of the ancient Eastern Christian Easter chant:

Christ is risen from the dead, trampling death by death,
and giving life to those in the tomb.

Here too we have echoes of an alternate theology of Original Sin. Strictly speaking, there is no such theological term in the Eastern system: an "original fall" perhaps, but not as a "sin" properly speaking, a guilt which each of us somehow shares. The sin of Adam and Eve is not seen so much as the cause of our dying, or even if it was seen as thus, this remains secondary to the fact that it is death itself that accounts for our sinfulness. True, "the wages of sin remain death", especially our eternal death, but death itself is the great unknown, and it is the fear of death that feeds our sinfulness. Out of our fear of and futile attempt to escape death we bring upon ourselves all the ills that afflict the human race. This was also a theme that was brilliantly expounded by the late Ernest Becker on purely psychological and sociological grounds in his 1974 Pulitzer Prize-winning book *The Denial of Death.*

Christians see that Jesus, in handing himself over totally in death, in total trust of the Father who seemed for a time to abandon him, experienced fully our often-repressed fear of death. He gave himself up entirely to the great abyss of the unknown, of *sheol*, the pit, the grave, the unknown netherworld of *Hades*, from whence no one had ever been known to return. But in doing so, Christ did not undergo the torments of hell, but instead "harrowed" or plundered hell of those destined to rise into eternal life. This is the great underlying theme of the Descent into Hell, however it be phrased or envisioned.

Nevertheless, despite this triumphal motif of ancient beliefs, death still haunts us. Faith, from this point of view, is not a set of sure answers to the mystery of death. Instead, it is a trustful, loving following of Jesus into, through, and out of the jaws of death.

Resurrection and Unitive Faith

Unfortunately, even when seen in the context of a "soul-less" Hebrew anthropology, the meaning of "resurrection" took on an ancient literalness that few people can take literally today. And, as we shall see (in the next chapter) few in the ancient non-Jewish world, or even in the Jewish world outside of the Pharisees, accepted it in any literal way. So then, are we to reduce the concept of "resurrection" to a mere metaphor of hope for eternal life?

If I have already spoken, somewhat hesitantly, of the mystical meanings of the words attributed to Jesus by the Gospel of John, it was partly with this question in mind. Perhaps, in some cases, these utterances are based on the actual remembered words of Jesus. But at the same time, I think they hardly need be. They are, in a way, the unspoken words of the risen Christ that nevertheless shout across the barriers of time and space. And I think we must face it, these barriers are very real.

Despite the proliferation of post-resurrection stories in the gospel— indeed, when examined more closely precisely in view of them—we can say that Jesus did not "rise" in the sense of returning to this world. Whatever he had hoped for, it was not some kind of resuscitation or miracle reversing the process of the grave that all, or even anyone, could see, such as reported in the raising of Lazarus. Even in the Scriptures, no one is claimed to have witnessed the resurrection of Jesus. Instead, they only experienced the Risen Christ. True, we have stories of an empty tomb, but these in themselves prove nothing, nor for that matter, would the finding of his corpse, as disconcerting as that might have been. What establishes the Resurrection as fact, as history, is something that goes beyond observable happenings, something that is, again, as the Russian philosopher Nicolas Berdeyev put it, "metahistorical", that is, transcending all time and space.

This is not to say that Mary Magdalene, the apostles, and the others did not really experience him in time, but we would have to understand it as an altogether other side of reality. Note that in almost all the gospel accounts, at first, none of them recognized him. Even Thomas, the doubting apostle, comes to his conclusion only after making the connection through the signs of the wounds. Although there is a certain continuity between this person and the Jesus they knew a few days before, he comes to them from another dimension in time and space—or from even beyond them—of which we know nothing.

Likewise, there is another curiosity regarding these accounts. In the earliest writings, Jesus is not spoken of as "rising from the death", but as being "*raised* from the dead"; in other words, in the passive sense as being acted upon by God, not as somehow asserting power in his own right. Only later, when his divinity becomes more clearly established, does the language switch more generally to the active voice. Most scripture scholars and theologians see the former as typical of the earliest mode of christological thought which is "adoptionist" in expression, tracing a line of ascent from his baptism where he is revealed as God's beloved, through Peter's confession and the Transfiguration, where he is revealed as "the Christ", to the Resurrection, by which he is lastly revealed to be God's "Son". Only the infancy narratives of Matthew and Luke and a few passages in the authentic Pauline epistles depart from this rule. So from this point of view it must be admitted that it is God who works the transformation upon Jesus. It is the Father himself who speaks the final word in the act of raising up Jesus from the dead—and from our perspective—brings about the final transformation of Jesus' own faith.

How so? Here we must examine another puzzle in the Johannine gospel. Although this gospel has even more detailed post-resurrection experiences than the others have, the language is remarkably different in one important respect. The synoptics see Jesus' glorification taking place by means of his Resurrection or, as in the case of Luke, by means of his Ascension. Instead, in John's gospel, in the long Last Supper discourse, Jesus is pictured as speaking of his *death* as being the moment of his glorification. So striking is this Johannine approach that it is almost as if his resurrection accounts are an afterthought, and that Jesus' being raised up in death on the cross is itself the manifestation of his glory!

This would be unexplainable unless we remember that it is in delivering himself over to death, voluntarily, in total abandonment to God, which constitutes Jesus as the Savior. "When I am lifted up from the earth, I will draw everyone to myself" (John 12:32). Again, in the account that John (11:45-52) gives us of the conspiracy to kill Jesus, the chief priests and Pharisees are depicted as being swayed by the argument that Jesus must be eliminated, not just to save their own influence, but for the sake of the whole nation, which they rightly saw as jeopardized if the Romans were to conclude that their limited Jewish home-rule was no longer viable. But then, as the author takes pains to note, this was to be even more true than their leaders suspected, for through his death would be gathered "together in unity the scattered children of God." No doubt this gospel emphasizes a particular irony here: through destroying Jesus the Jewish leaders did in fact destroy their nation and its temple cult, bringing about a new *diaspora* situation, wherein Jewish Christians now went out to spread the gospel to the nations.

Someone may rightly object that none of this concerns verifiable changes in Jesus himself, but theological reflections on the image of Jesus after his resurrection, now perceived as the glorified Christ. No doubt this is true, yet to admit this is not to say that this is not what precisely happened. The claim that God had raised Jesus from the dead remains controversial, to say the least. But in itself, a miracle of resurrection, like that claimed in John's gospel regarding Lazarus, and oddly ignored by the synoptic writers, would prove nothing. It would remain, perhaps, merely a curiosity, or at best, a possible motive or catalyst towards belief. Contrary to the old saying, seeing is not necessarily the same as believing.

There is a remarkable contemporary example. Only a few years ago there was something of an uproar when a Jewish scholar, Pincus Lapide, entertained the possibility that Jesus actually did rise from the dead or at least that the belief that he did might represent an "authentic Jewish experience of faith" (see Hans Küng, *Eternal Life?*, p. 275, note 17). To my knowledge, Professor Lapide did not later become a Christian. The logic of faith may indeed assert that "if Christ was not raised, then your faith is in vain" (I Corinthians 15:17), but this statement can not be extended to claim that even if we are convinced that Christ has risen, then faith must automatically follow. Belief in the resurrection of Jesus and a living faith are two different things. The one has to do with what actually happened at some past point in time: the other has to do with its effects in subsequent history.

This comment in some way takes us back to the differences between the earthly or historical Jesus and the historic Jesus as one who influences history or as the "Christ of Faith". Jesus of Nazareth, the Jewish religious leader who lived and died in the Roman occupied province of Palestine during the reign of Tiberius Caesar was hardly noted by the historians of his time. Yet this would-be—at least in the eyes of his followers—Jewish Messiah was to be proclaimed before long, eventually even by the successors of these same emperors, as "the Christ", the "Son of God", the "King of Kings" and "Lord of Lords", the *"Pantocrator"* of the universe!

In this chapter I have tried to show how the faith that Jesus had in his own mission led him, despite the horrors that faced him, to give his life up entirely into the hands of God. In doing so, his faith was transformed into victory. But just how this transformation of Jesus' own faith in God and in the resurrection became the foundation for *our* faith in the risen Christ is another story, one that I can only begin to attempt to sketch out in the chapter that follows.

Chapter 6

The Universal Savior

How did the faith of the man known as Jesus of Nazareth become a faith in that same person being the Messiah/Christ who is our "Savior" and "Son of God"?

Here we must ponder the problem of how a particular faith, necessarily limited by the bonds of culture and religious tradition, can somehow be transformed so that these bonds can be transcended to become a universal faith. One senses that beneath the remaining limitations of the cultural context of their faith and beliefs, the really great mystics and saints harbor within themselves a certain universal wisdom and vision that transcends the all too narrow bonds of even the highest religious expression. I suspect that the same is true of those who have passed through the dark night of martyrdom, but for most of these, we simply have no record of their thoughts on the other side of death. It is no longer simply a matter of new wine stretching the old wineskins beyond their capacity: it is more like an overwhelming fountain inundating all that stands before it or like the stream envisioned by Ezekiel (47:1-12) that grows in volume as it leaves its source. So it is with the power unleashed by belief in the Resurrection of Jesus.

From Messiah to Universal Christ

There have been more than enough theories that have attempted to explain this transformation. Here I am not speaking of those theories that would try to explain away the Resurrection of Jesus as wishful thinking or a hallucination of the apostles. Granted the possibility of such dubious "revelations", they would still hardly explain the successful transformation of a Jewish messianic sect into a world religion. Those who begin by emphasizing the readiness of many people in those days to believe in the return of all sorts of people from the dead—even Herod thought Jesus might be John the Baptist resurrected—only undercut their own line of argument. For if people really were rising from the dead with such presumed regularity, how is it that Jesus of Nazareth, put to death as a political criminal by the representative of imperial Rome, would become, within three centuries of his execution, not only the central cult figure of that same empire, but even of many other peoples intent on the destruction of the same empire?

Even presupposing the reality of the resurrection of Jesus, at least in the sense that we allowed in the previous chapter as a "metahistorical" event, neither disprovable in itself nor provable by ordinary evidence, we still have to explain how belief in a resurrected Jesus became a faith in the universal Christ.

Most theories—some of them admittedly connected with disbelief in the resurrection, as well as those seeking to trace the lines of legitimate theological development—have given St. Paul most of the credit (or blame) for the transformation that took place.

The reason for this is not hard to see. Saul of Tarsus, the name under which he was first known, was not one of the original disciples, being neither among "the twelve" nor even part of the larger body of close followers that we are told numbered seventy-two. Yet, as an early convert who saw his appointed task as that of an apostle to the gentiles—although he seems always to have first approached the local Jewish community wherever he went—it is only natural that his version of the teaching of Jesus would soon blossom into a religion centered on a universal Christ. Nonetheless, it still remains to be determined just how, in theological terms, this change came about. Perhaps about a half-a-dozen possible factors were involved.

I should also make it clear at this time that my exploration of these factors does not mean that any of them or even all of them are themselves the reason one might believe that Jesus is, in fact, who one holds him to be. The believer obviously holds what he believes as truth in its own right. My recounting of various explanations, or my attempt at an explanation of my own, should only to be taken as contributing factors. Ultimately, a faith of this kind remains a gift or "grace".

The first and the most obvious factor centers on the idea of disappointed apocalyptic expectations. According to this opinion, when the second coming of Christ failed to materialize, the early Christians simply shifted their emphasis from the messianic kingdom to the person of Jesus himself. To paraphrase Albert Schweitzer, Jesus came preaching the Kingdom of God and (after that) the Apostles, especially Paul, preached Jesus. This is, of course, too simple, but there is still much truth in it. Even if from the beginning of his apostolate Paul presents Jesus as a universal savior, there can be no question that at first Paul also expected Christ's imminent return. Only gradually do we see Paul shifting his perspective to a situation where the second coming, still delayed, ceases to be a central motif. Indeed some of these later writings, the so-called "pastoral epistles" to Timothy and Titus, and certain of the "captivity epistles" (those to the Colossians and Ephesians, in particular) differ so markedly in their vocabulary and themes that they are often ascribed by modern scholars to disciples of Paul instead of to Paul himself.

If this shift in emphasis is true for Paul or for those who wrote in his name, and who represent the earliest Christian writers, the same transformation might be expected in much of the rest of the New Testament, including the gospels themselves. In these latter, as documents claiming to picture Jesus as he was, this same shift in emphasis away from expectation of the imminent return of Christ is evident as well. According to Mark's gospel, the earliest of the four, Jesus is an apocalyptic preacher of the end time—although never simply that. The same is largely true in Matthew, although a new emphasis on the "gathering" (the *qahal* or *ekklesia*) modifies this emphasis somewhat.

But when we come to Luke, we find an approach, despite Luke's repetition of the "last days" theme, which is more concentrated on the *person* of Jesus in contrast to the earlier emphasis on his message. And even as far as Luke's message goes, it already shows a strong tendency toward bringing about the realization of God's kingdom in *this* world in the *present* time rather than simply preparing ourselves for a kingdom yet to come. This is even more true when it comes to John's gospel, where the warning of the "Last Days" all but entirely disappears.

In sum, there is, even within the collection of writings that form the New Testament, ample evidence of a development of doctrine concerning the identity of Jesus Christ. The Hebrew term *Meshiach* was not simply translated into the Greek *Christos*. Instead, the long-awaited, and still largely unfulfilled expectations of a Jewish messiah are for the most part sidestepped and superseded by the proclamation of universal salvation through the mediation of and even through the person of "the Lord Jesus Christ". There can be no doubt the failure of history itself to come to a sudden end, which Jesus' first followers seemed to have assumed that he had predicted, had a lot to do with this change.

Yet there is another factor much more at work here than simply failed apocalyptic expectations, and it has even greater implications than the gradual abandonment of a frustrated Jewish messianism. Again, it still has a lot to do with the transformation of the expectations of a second coming of Christ into the acceptance of the present state of affairs as being already the realization, at least in part, of God's kingdom and the beginning of a new age. Nowhere is this more evident than in Paul's use of the term "Lord" in the way he applies it to Jesus.

That this word (*Kyrios* in Greek) is ambiguous in itself—indeed many earthly figures have been, and still are in some cultures, addressed as "Lord", even as Jesus sometimes is addressed in the gospels—does not solve the matter. But when Paul used this term he did so deliberately with more than just the ordinary reverential overtones. In fact, *Kyrios* was the term selected by the Greek-speaking Jewish Septuagint translators to replace the Hebrew word *Adonai* which in turn was used in those times to substitute for the sacred name *Yahweh*. So in his use of the title *Kyrios*, Paul is in effect designating Christ as being (at least in some way) equal to God.

True, Paul never uses the generic term *Theos,* especially with the article (*ho Theos*—literally "the God" in Greek, but generally translated without the article), directly of Jesus, but in at least one place (Titus 2:13) the same term is so closely associated with Christ that there can be little doubt that for Paul (or whoever wrote this letter) the Lord Jesus Christ is truly divine. The same goes for the authors of the Epistle to the Hebrews and II Peter, and of course, for John's gospel.

Some would caution that Paul in his earliest writings retains something of the primitive Christian predilection far describing Jesus' exaltation as "Lord" as a *result* of his resurrection, hence that Paul still thought Christ's divinity as somewhat qualified in some way. But on the other hand, at least when we survey the Pauline writings as a whole, they show a marked tendency toward thinking of Jesus' lordship as the recognition of his return to his former state as God's son. The clearest evidence for this is not any Pauline use of the term *Theos* as applied to Christ, but more in his statement in Philippians: (2:6) that his [Christ's] state was divine, yet he did not cling to his equality with God..."

In all this there can be no doubt that Paul and his co-workers introduced a major alteration in, or even what seems to be a serious deviation from, Jewish monotheism into the Christian concept of God, one that holds that Jesus is not only "Son of God" in the Hebrew sense of the term—one chosen by God and designated to a special task—but instead as the very *incarnation* of God. Once that bold step has been taken, then, as we shall soon see, there is no limit to the claims that might be made in his name.

But first, before we go on to that, we should look at two more factors that are often advanced as explanations as to how the failed "Messiah" became the triumphant "Lord Jesus Christ". One of these additional factors is the claim that Paul, still desiring to spread the essence of Jewish monotheism to the rest of the world, promoted the idea of replacing the legalistic piety of his early pharisaism with theological elaborations based on ideas derived from various Greek "mystery cults", as well as mixing certain Gnostic rites and speculations with biblical themes. Hence the simple Jewish rites of repentance and purification become the symbolic death and rebirth of baptism and the Passover *Seder* with its *barakah* or blessing of the bread and cup become the mystical sharing of the body and the blood of Christ in the Eucharistic meal. In these sacramental rituals the simple memory of Jesus' life was transformed into a means of corporate identification with the exalted Lord who in turn shares his glorified life with his followers here on earth.

That such an adaptation to the ritualized religious mentality of late antiquity would find ready acceptance, when various mystery cults were sweeping the Roman Empire, seems likely enough. And certainly, for one who really believes that Jesus was raised from the dead and lives eternally in a state of restored divinity, such a ritualization is altogether logical, even if not without its dangers—as Jesus himself had pointed out in his own critique of both the temple cult and of pharisaism. But neither does this adaptation to the popular religious mentality explain why it is that Christianity should emerge victorious over the other cults, some of which, for example Mithraism, may have been originally more widespread.

Of course there is always the moral factor to be considered. Christianity, and the rigorous ethical code it represented, in contrast to the moral decay of the late empire, proved, it may be said, a real attraction to good people of high principle who were looking for a sounder foundation for the natural virtues than paganism, at its best, once fostered. That Jewish proselytism had been able to make significant inroads among such people, despite its ritual exclusivity, shows that the world was becoming ripe for such a challenge as Christian morality. But again, this was only another factor, and in itself probably not the decisive one. In fact, the ethical reform espoused by emperor Marcus Aurelius included the persecution of Christians because in that philosopher-emperor's eyes, Christian morals were not rigorous enough! Neither would a turn to moral rigorism, any more than a turn to ritualism, in itself really explain why Jesus of Nazareth would himself become worshipped as God.

Perhaps this is the place to mention one other aspect that might be seen as related to this longing for a higher moral tone. It has often been alleged that early Christianity found its strongest backing among the slaves and lower classes of society, in a word, among people yearning for a better lot in life. No doubt this impression is reinforced by the lingering of paganism among many prominent Roman citizens—naturally conservative due to their privileged positions in society—for some time after Christianity was legalized and had begun to make even more serious inroads into the old ways. But at least one recent historical-sociological study has indicated that contrary to this impression, Christianity had made some of its most significant gains among the upper classes, particularly due to the influence of women. Perhaps too they saw much to be gained to their advantage.

It should also be noted that on a whole, the rural populations were among the last to be converted. Although the term *"pagani"* originally had nothing directly to do with religion—it simply meant the "country-folk"— we also know that in such a setting, the idea of a universal Christ or savior, along with monotheism in general, tended to encounter greatest resistance from the rural populations with their many gods.

Here, no doubt, a final factor, a more directly political one, comes into play. Thus the decisive effect of imperial power exercised by Constantine the Great, his legalization of and later official establishment of Christianity, and most of all, his and his successors' interventions in the formulation of Christian doctrines. That Christianity should become so widespread throughout the empire, despite repeated persecutions, is a remarkable enough fact. That an emperor, who was in fact not a practicing Christian (at least not fully so until his death-bed baptism) should be the decisive factor leading to the formation of an official "orthodoxy" is even more significant. If Constantine's ascendancy to the throne in 313 needed the legitimization from Christians, the precarious unity of this vast empire demanded the unity of Christianity itself.

That the divine status as applied to Jesus Christ happened at such an early time as the preaching of Paul does not mean, however, that it was accepted completely at face value right away. There were, in fact, many competing interpretations as to how Jesus was considered to be divine, and up to the time of Constantine's ascendancy, no single explanation had prevailed. In fact, shortly before his coming to power, the doctrine of Arius, a priest-theologian in Alexandria, had gained major popularity in almost all areas of the Christian world, even to the extent that it has been estimated that if all the bishops at that time had been asked and felt free to declare their opinions, "Arianism", which accorded Jesus a quasi but not fully divine status, would have prevailed. But thanks to the emperor, this was not to be.

In 325, at Nicea, Constantine convened and personally presided over the first of what became known as a series of "ecumenical councils" that formulated, in rapid succession, a body of dogmas defining the divinity of Jesus, the nature of God as a trinity, and the dual divine and human natures of Christ. But to all these factors, I would like to add one more.

What we see here is, I would contend, a final "universalization" of the faith of Jesus. Not a universalization in the sense that some of the above theories would envision—a deliberate manipulation of the memory of Jesus by his disappointed messianic followers, or a calculated effort by Paul to create a "Judaism for Gentiles", or even an opportunistic move by the imperial powers to capitalize on what they could no longer resist. Instead, what I am talking about is the universalization of Jesus' own religious consciousness, his own beliefs, and his own faithful trust in God.

This may sound strange at first, but ideas have their own momentum —often well beyond the initial awareness of their own originators. The story is told of Albert Einstein, that well after his proposal of the theories of both special and general relativity, that a society was formed by his admirers to propagate and advance the applications of his thought, partly by awarding prizes to the most outstanding disciples. Einstein himself was persuaded to act as a judge. But after examining one particularly brilliant competitor, the great man of science sent a note to the officers of the society, complaining that he had no idea of what this young man was talking about!

Some, of course, would say that this would have been Jesus' own comment about the ideas that Paul would advance in Jesus' name. Perhaps so: but is that to say that Paul was wrong? Consider this: just as Einstein himself can be said to have started a revolution, not only Jesus but Paul himself can be said to have started a "school" of theological interpretation that outstripped its founder. Thus the ascended "Lord Jesus" of the early Paul becomes even more expansively the universal "Christ".

Paul advanced, at a very early date, beyond the primitive formulations of Jesus' exaltation to Lordship, to recognition of his pre-existent divinity. But was even this all Paul's own doing? This is not only clear in the letter to the Philippians, but also in the letter to the Colossians, where we find what appears to a be a quotation from a hymn-like canticle that extols Christ as:

> ...the image of the invisible God,
> the firstborn of all creation...
> all things were created through him and for him.
> He is before all things,
> and in him all things hold together.
> (Colossians 1:15-17)

In this passage, we find a strong parallel to the prologue of John's gospel. But there is something more. Both this hymn and the Johannine tradition draw from the late Old Testament image of divine wisdom (see especially Wisdom 7:22-8:11), but instead of recasting this tradition in terms of the Greek concept of the *Logos* (divine "reason" or "The Word"), as the prototype of all creation, much as did John. (Note especially the parallel between John 1:1 and Genesis 1:1) The difference is mostly in that the Pauline mode of thought leaps ahead with its focus not on the beginning so much as the end. In this way Christ becomes, as the later Pauline tradition was to say in so many words, what we might describe as being "coextensive" with the universe. Glorified by the Father, Jesus is now revealed (through his church) as the "fullness" (*plêrôma*) of him who fills the universe in all its parts" (Ephesians 1:23) or in the latest revision of *The New American Bible* translation, "the fullness of the one who fills all things in every way." Yet even these later Pauline expressions seem to echo, in somewhat different language, where we already find early as I Corinthians when Paul tells us that the redeemed cosmos will be handed over by Christ to his Father so that "God may become all in all" (I Corinthians 15:28).

Clearly, the vision of the glorified Christ presented by Paul and his disciples far outstrips in its universality anything imagined in the synoptic gospels, and even, to some extent, that presented somewhat later by John. But in all this, could not we, or Paul—or even Jesus himself—have been wrong?

The Aims of Jesus

What really were the aims or intentions of Jesus of Nazareth? In terms of what we can find in the synoptics, or even from a more careful reading of John, Jesus' own ambitions seem to have been considerably less than those of his followers. What appears to have begun as a mission to ready his own people for the coming of God's kingdom, or at most, less apocalyptically, to actuate the reign of God here and now in the hearts and in the lives of his followers has become a movement far more universal and ambitious in its scope than anything Jesus may have, humanly speaking, possibly imagined. And, as we have already seen, the transformation that took place may have been due, to begin with, to the fact that if Jesus was expecting the imminent coming of God's kingdom, that in this he was completely mistaken.

This paradox invites further reflection and, again, a further comparison with Albert Einstein. This great and much honored genius of modern thought is considered by many scientists today to have been completely wrong, not about relativity as such, but about the role of chance in the universe and the truth of Heisenberg's "uncertainty principle". "I refuse", Einstein was to say, "to believe that God plays dice!" And consequently he was unable, in his later years, to follow the development of much of the cosmological thought that owed so much to his early insights and inspiration. (See Stephen Hawking, 1988.) As a result, those who limit themselves to following Einstein's insights, as great as they are, prove themselves almost as hampered to cope with modern discoveries as those who would limit their understanding to the clockwork model of the universe proposed by Newton.

In the same way, do we not hamper ourselves by placing all our faith in Jesus, or even more, to being restricted to duplicating Jesus' own faith? If Jesus was, for example, wrong about the imminent arrival of "The Kingdom of God", do we not end in committing the same error as the early Christians at Thessalonika, who in their anticipation of the sudden end of the world, much to Paul's dismay, seemed to think that they need not contribute to the world—indeed, that the world apparently owed them a living? Paul's answer to that was "if a man will not work, neither let him eat!" (II Thessalonians 3:10). In the same way, should we not wonder if it might not have been possible that early Christianity took a wrong turn, not only about the imminent end of the world and the return of Christ, but also, in reaction to those failed expectations, about the identity of Jesus himself?

To answer this question, look at it this way. Even if Jesus really was wrong in anticipating an early end to history, is this to say that the rest of his ideas were thereby invalid? Or is it not possible to say that such were the power of his ideas that in fact a new era indeed has arrived? Did not the interpretation of traditional biblical religion that he himself embodied prove to be so radical a reinterpretation so as to in effect become the beginning of a complete transformation of religious consciousness for the whole human race? (Notice, I say the "beginning"—for the process is far from complete, even among those of us who claim to be "Christians".)

Or, again, consider this. The earthly Jesus may have been the embodiment of Jewish piety at its holiest, totally given over to the will of God, totally committed to the honor of God's name, and totally, even radically, partisan for the holiness of God's temple—especially if by "holiness" (Hebrew *kadosh*) is understood especially in the sense of an apartness or separation from the profane. If so, then rather than seeing him as fundamentally opposed to the Pharisees (an impression given by the gospel writers that may reflect the situation between his followers and the Pharisees only later on) Jesus' disruptive incursions into the Jerusalem temple, with his angry reactions to the buying and selling activity, must followed in the footsteps of the great Hebrew prophets who were sent to primarily to their *own* nation, even though much of the world now treasures these prophecies as revelations to the whole human race? So too, can we not also say that his predictions of the future, like those of the prophets before him, also turned out to be something less than the literal truth, yet, at the same time, in an uncanny way typical of other events that were yet to come?

In the same way, even if Jesus only reluctantly allowed his mission to reach out, on a few rare occasions, to "gentiles", his tolerance for sinners and his preaching to the outcasts among his people was a harbinger of a much broader movement than the reformation of Israel. This may not have been because of any explicit instructions—unless the command to go out and baptize "all nations" is taken literally as a record of the actual words of Jesus (which few scholars would admit today). Rather it is a result of the implicit openness that Jesus showed to those Jews and Samaritans who existed beyond the pale of the law, and on a few occasions, even to pagans of good will, that early on Christianity would explicitly call itself "catholic" (*kata* plus *holos*, that is, regarding the whole or "all-embracing") because, in the words of Cyril of Jerusalem it would attempt to reach the whole world, to teach all of Christ's message to all people, to forgive all sins and promote every kind of virtue.

True, there is no solid exegetical foundation to claiming that in any sense Jesus understood himself to be founding a "church" as we understand the word today. The word *ekklesia* occurs only twice in the gospels, both times in Matthew. We can guess that behind this Greek word stands the Hebrew (or at least the Aramaic equivalent of) *qahal*, meaning a group that is "called together", clearly reflecting the situation of the infant congregation some years later. The first example, of course, is the famous "confession" of Peter (Matthew 16:18) related as a response to the crucial question, "Who do people say that I am?" It points to the stability of his following in resisting the encroachment of the outside world with the promise that "the gates of hell shall not overcome it." The second gospel use of the word is in Matthew 18:17, where in reference to settling disputes within the local congregations, it would seem to have an even more limited and local meaning.

So then what about the famous command to "go out and proclaim the good news to all creation ... " (Mark 16:15ff.)? This ending to Mark's gospel (the whole block of verses 9-20 is missing from some very early manuscripts) is widely recognized as a second, later ending added to Mark's original. Hence it is obviously second or even third level material according to the Biblical Commission analysis, while the parallel passages in Matthew and Luke are most likely a borrowing from this later addition. It clearly represents a later stage of apostolic consciousness from what his disciples first understood their task to be—either that or "all creation" here has to be understood like the French *toute le monde*—not literally "the whole world" but more like "everyone in sight"—thus the change "to all nations" in

Matthew proves that this expansion of missionary consciousness was growing at a pace that is truly surprising.

But with that exception, what we see in the New Testament writings taken across the board is a slowly dawning realization that the message of Jesus has to be taken out of its strictly Jewish context and "universalized" for the sake of the whole world. But note that this is not a conscious program, a plan or a plot of some sort. Instead, when we look at the real story of this transformation, even given in a somewhat dramatized and idealized form, as in The Acts of the Apostles, we find that instead of an unmitigated outpouring of missionary zeal, there is at first a certain hesitancy and even, in some quarters, a stubborn resistance to any expansion of membership in the group of followers, particularly when it comes to gentile or non-Jewish people. So while Luke's parallel passage to Mark's epilogue, like Matthew's, suggests an immediate mission "to all nations" or "peoples", Luke's second version of the same in Acts (1:8) not only slows the process down somewhat, even if in geographical instead of ethnic terms—beginning first in Jerusalem but then to "Judea and Samaria" next and only then "to the ends of the earth."

Although the Samaritans were seen as foreigners in Jewish eyes, to a gentile like Luke, they must have seemed like half-Jews—which was more or less true. So even here Luke's new geographical approach appears to reflect an original policy of going out to the "ends of the earth" but probably only with the object of reaching scattered Jews. Thus we are being set up by Luke in a way that we'll be in for a big surprise. After his accounts of the first activities and sufferings of the apostles in Jerusalem in their mission to fellow Jews, we are introduced to some upsetting new developments for the conservative followers in Jerusalem.

First, Philip the "deacon"—who was supposed to stay in Jerusalem "waiting on tables", not preaching—baptizes a group of Samaritans, and even worse, an Ethiopian eunuch who offered him a ride along the Gaza road. So Peter and John have to travel up to Samaria to legitimate Philip's rash move there, while the Ethiopian is long gone back to Africa. As for the Jerusalem community, perhaps they just pretended that the Gaza road incident didn't happen or hoped that the eunuch had already been a Jew.

Next, Peter himself becomes carried away while on a mission to the coastal cities and baptizes a Roman centurion and his whole household. This is too much for the people back in Jerusalem when they hear of it, so Peter has to go back and defend himself to the rest with an appeal to the Holy Spirit, including a thrice repeated vision that abolishes all distinctions between "clean" (*kosher*) and unclean food, and by implication, between Jew and gentile as well.

But even then, the issue was not fully resolved, so later, after the firebrand Pharisee Saul is converted and becomes Paul the Apostle, we see the whole issue raised again, this time to be settled, as it were, by the first Christian church "council" held in Jerusalem about the year 50. There is dissension in the ranks to be sure, but even here, Luke may have altered the story somewhat. An agreement of sorts is reached: gentiles are to be accorded equal status with Jews in the fledgling church, providing they keep a few major points of Jewish law for harmony's sake.

But the facts of the real story, as are more than hinted by the rest of Acts and by the early Pauline epistles, tell a less idyllic tale than at first meets the eye. That the message of Jesus was at first simply called "The Way" (Acts 9:2) and its first followers were called "the brotherhood" (Acts 2:42), or "Nazareans", and eventually became known, possibly by the mid-century, as "Christians" (Acts 11:26); all this only partially reflects the long process of the movement's slow separation from its parent religion and its gradual universalization.

There is also evidence from early Galilean rabbinic documents that the followers of Jesus, while still attending the synagogues, were already being called "*minim*" by the orthodox (apparently from the Hebrew word *min*, denoting a "portion" or "party"). Apparently a deliberate attempt was being made to exclude them, but that such were the number of his followers, at least in Galilee, that it could no longer be a simple matter of exclusion from the synagogues or excommunication. The followers of Jesus seem to have been forced to form their own congregations as it were, not by choice but by default. There is also an increasing amount of archeological evidence of early Jewish-Christian enclaves scattered throughout Israel, even as far south as Hebron.

So it seems that the difficulties that the original followers of Jesus, who saw themselves entirely as Jews within Judaism, but who instead soon found themselves considered a schismatic sect, only served at first to strengthen their resolve to redouble their efforts to be considered as orthodox Jews and to see their following of Jesus as a fulfillment of the authentic Jewish tradition. This was the group that identified with James, "the brother of the Lord". For these people, it was not so much the decision made in Jerusalem in the year 50 to admit gentiles into the fellowship, but the destruction of Jerusalem by the Roman army in 70, that did more to separate the followers of Jesus from the rest of Judaism than did any other event.

In fact, there are those who see this disaster, along with the aftermath of the *Bar Kochba* revolt in 135, as the real beginning of modern "Judaism" as well. Be that as it may, it was the better part of four centuries before the distinctively Jewish form of Christianity died out in the Holy Land. Indeed some vestiges of it persist today in the non-Byzantine churches of the Near East, particularly in the Syrian Rite and in the Maronite Rite in Lebanon, and among Chaldean Christians in Iraq, where a variation of the Aramaic language of Jesus' own time survives in limited liturgical use.

At the same time, a somewhat different strain of Christianity developed under the impetus of the Apostle Paul. Instead of stressing continuity with Judaism, this ex-rabbinical student, from the first flush of his sudden conversion, took a predominantly "supplantational" line. According to Paul (see especially Romans chapters 9-11), his ancestral people, the Jews, still remain special to God, but as far as the old law or the old covenant is concerned, it is dead—"put to death" with the earthly Jesus on the Cross. A new covenant, a new law of love and grace, is born with the resurrection of the "Christ" Jesus, now revealed fully as Lord. In this way the tentative and halting steps begun by Philip and Peter are vindicated and multiplied by Paul and his missionary band with vigor that the left the mother church in Jerusalem dumbfounded and alarmed. Christianity was rapidly ceasing to be Jewish.

Could Jesus have possibly foreseen this? If one reads history backwards and, against all prevailing scholarship, takes the closing "missionary" passages of the synoptic gospels as actual records of the words of Jesus—and these in turn, as expressions of the divine Christ who knew from the very beginning how it was all to turn out, then, of course, there is no problem with all this. It was only the residual Jewish stubbornness of the other disciples that stood in the way.

But there is precious little evidence in the gospels that Jesus really did have any such program in mind. True, he did express some amazement and admiration regarding the "faith" of those pagans who persisted in seeking his healing powers. According to John's gospel (chapter 5) Jesus actively courted the attention of a Samaritan woman who in turn would draw her fellow townsfolk to hear him. Yet, not long after, to those Greeks who requested the apostle Philip to arrange an interview, Jesus seems to have given short shrift (John 12:20ff.).

At most, perhaps, Jesus envisioned a reform of Judaism that in turn would reach out—as it already was in its more liberal forms of proselytism —with a truly universal mission to the rest of the world. But as far as we can see, Jesus would have been grateful even if he could have kept his Galilean following intact, much more if he could have moved the Judaean hierarchy and its following. He succeeded in neither.

What Jesus clearly intended, the revitalization of the Jewish faith under the call of the demands of God's Kingdom, turned out have been a complete failure. That he might have possibly envisioned a renewed Judaism as a source of moral renewal in the world is not beyond possibility, but again, he would not live to see that result in any substantial form. Instead, after his tragic and untimely death, what resulted, despite Luke's somewhat revisionist account in Acts, was a break-away sect that has painfully transformed itself into a major contender in the arena of the world's would-be universal faiths.

Seeking a Universal Faith

Here we have a paradox! Jesus, who appears to have experienced a truly "unitive" degree of faith in God, may never have reached, on this side of the grave, a truly "universalized" faith—one, without further development, capable of being the nucleus of a truly world-wide religion. Instead, it was precisely in his failure even to convert the bulk of his own people that the seeds of a universal Christianity were born.

This is a shocking assertion, but consider the alternative. Let us suppose, to the contrary, Jesus had been an unqualified success. To take a more recent example, consider the expanding aims of the Rev. Sun Myung Moon, founder of the organization he called "The Holy Spirit Association for the Unification of World Christianity", but more often called simply "the Unification Church" since Moon seems to have gradually broadened his goal to uniting *all* religions, not just Christianity. This seems to be a result of Moon's claim that Jesus was a failure at becoming the Messiah because he was killed before he could begin the real work of reforming the human race. According to Moon, this reform would have involved Jesus' eventual marriage and the founding of a perfect family to set a new divine pattern for the restoration of the human race (which rather sounds like the final fantasy in the Kanzantzakis novel, *The Last Temptation of Christ*). But suppose that this happened and that the whole world responded to this revelation of "The Divine Principle" (the title of Moon's own doctrinal testament). Interestingly, Moon did not claim, as his critics charged, to be *the* Messiah himself. Instead he claimed that he would have been proven to be the Messiah if his doctrine were to succeed in converting the world! But if he had, what then?

Perhaps it is difficult if not foolish to speculate about such things. Yet it raises profound questions. Did God really intend Jesus to die? Or, if he had to die like the rest of us, why not a gentle passing away at a ripe old age—for example, like Gautama the Buddha? Did the will of God the Father, or an angry sense of divine justice, really demand that his "Son" be cruelly, bloodily "sacrificed" on a cross to appease God's wrath, as one line of Christian theology has taken to explain this apparently tragic miscarriage of human justice?

Of course, in terms of human memory, there is nothing like an unjustly afflicted violent death to immortalize a person. Socrates would be little remembered today outside of his role in Plato's *Dialogues*, and his memory not nearly as hallowed, were it not for his forced suicide. Lincoln has gone down in history as a martyr for human rights much more than as the tragic, brooding figure that oversaw what was, until World War I came along, the bloodiest war in human history. John F. Kennedy—who alive at the time can forget that day? —then his brother, Robert, then Martin Luther King! The list goes on and on.

Here indeed is the *true* "Divine Principle"—the "paschal" mystery, the fact that it is only in dying that we live, and that "he who would save his life shall lose it, where he who loses it...shall live." The seed must die before it can bear fruit. The religions that set out consciously to convert the whole world through messages of peace and prosperity are probably the least likely to succeed and those that would attempt to do it through fire and sword even less likely to do so. Self-proclaimed "messiahs" are doomed to fall flat on their face. And so are successful ones!

Luke, in The Acts of the Apostles (5:34ff.) tells us that the more liberal Jewish scholar and member of the Sanhedrin, Gamaliel, gave some sage advice about would-be messiahs—leave them alone or let them be. If spurious, their movements will come to nothing. But on the other hand, if sent by God, who are we to resist them—as well as God?

It is a little more than ironic that Gamaliel's most well-known disciple did not follow his master's advice at first. Saul of Tarsus took an active part in the killing of the first Christian martyr, Stephen, and then went on to become one of the chief agents of persecution. Only after his traumatic conversion did he become the apostle, Paul. Almost inevitably, the blood of martyrs becomes the seed of faith. In this we follow in the footsteps of Jesus himself.

When all is said and done, it appears that the lesson of the life and death of Jesus should teach us more than one thing. Foremost, even if the most overlooked, is the eventual collapse of all human plans, agendas, paradigms, beliefs—even, to some extent, of faith itself—in the face of the unfathomable mystery of God. This is why I quoted the long passage I did at the beginning of chapter five. As tentative and as nuanced as it may be, it contains an awful truth. And that truth is that not only do we have to die to the sureness that we are somehow called or singled out by God before we can become the instruments that God wishes us to be, but that even our ideas, our comforting beliefs about God must also die before we can experience the fullness of the truth. Not only that, but only through the radical divestment of the "unitive" state itself, through the sundering of our own unity by death, can a full *universalization* of our faith take place. For it is no longer our faith that is at stake, but our very selves, and it is only when they both die, together, that resurrection to true life can take place!

Chapter 7

Faith in Christ: A Christological Postscript

In the preceding chapters that made up most of this short book, I have given my own personal version of the life of Jesus of Nazareth, one based on a largely psychological theory of faith development with the assistance of contemporary New Testament scholarship. In much the same vein, I have also tried to show that, given belief in his Resurrection, there is a natural progression from belief in Jesus as the rejected Jewish Messiah to the Lord Christ who is a universal redeemer of humanity, indeed, of the whole universe. Loosely speaking, these chapters have centered more on what is sometimes called, at least by Christian theologians, a "soteriology", that is, an approach to Jesus of Nazareth that focuses on his function or mission as "Savior" (*sôtêr* in Greek) of humanity.

In this final chapter or epilogue—really, just a postscript in contrast to the vast amount of study this subject deserves—I will attempt to reflect, however briefly, on christology as such, which is that branch of theology that focuses primarily the personal identity of Jesus, not simply as the Savior, but as the "Son of God" in the full Christian understanding of that term.

Of course, the two areas, soteriology and christology, are closely intertwined. The latter exists to explain the former. But theologically speaking, there is a huge gap, on the one hand, between acclaiming this savior as the "Servant-Son of God" in the Hebrew sense of the words, as contrasted, on the other hand, to the full-blown Christian confession that this same Jesus is "God from true God, Light from true Light" (Council of Nicea, 325 AD). Although the doctrine of the Trinity supposedly kept the identity of Jesus as "Son" distinct from the "Father", once this belief in the preexisting divinity of Christ became defined, another very difficult problem has taken its place, that of maintaining his humanity along with his divinity. This is what is often called "the christological problem" or sometimes, alternately, the "Chalcedonian problem" because, according to the classic statement of the Council of Chalcedon (451 AD), this "one and the same person", Jesus Christ, is "consubstantial [i.e., of the same nature] with us in his humanity, and consubstantial with God in his divinity".

But instead of settling the problem, Chalcedon only restated it in more exact terms. History has shown that the problem of keeping the two statements about Christ in balance has been all but impossible, while the mystery of how he can be both fully human as well as divine has proved all but insolvable.

The effort to maintain this delicate balance or seeming contradiction has unfortunately led toward a popular view that splits the single reality of Jesus Christ into the mere semblance of a man (Jesus) who is the visible form of a totally divine person called "Christ". One of the major aims of this book has been to do away with this caricature by picturing him as a real, suffering, and believing human being. The purpose of this postscript or epilogue is to ask or suggest briefly how we might also look upon him as divine or as the self-revelation of God.

Many contemporary theologians have suggested that a major part of the problem has been in assuming that we really know what God is like, and that, as a consequence, we have projected onto the figure of Jesus certain ideas that are incompatible with the human condition as we generally know it to be—for example, the idea that he had to have known everything, and that, as a consequence, he had no necessity for faith. These theologians suggest that if Jesus Christ really is "the image of the unseen God" (Colossians 1:12) then we should instead start the other way around and begin with what we see in Jesus and only then draw our conclusions about God.

However, as much I am inclined to agree with that approach—and I will come back to it—I am even more inclined to agree with a few other theologians who suggest that perhaps even more our trouble lies in supposing that we have correctly understood human nature to begin with. As strange as this suggestion might seem—after all, don't we experience being human first hand?—I think there is much merit in the suggestion. I say this for two reasons: first, because I think that we have in the past misunderstood the biblical view of human nature, wrongly reading into it ideas derived from certain ancient Greek philosophies; and, second, because modern science has revealed a different view of human nature, one that in some ways is much closer to the ancient biblical view. For despite the apparent contradiction between the scriptural understanding of creation and the modern scientific theories of evolution, there are some surprising convergences. Nowhere is this more striking than when it comes to our view of ourselves.

The Bible and the Evolution of Human Nature

Too often we have assumed, in the mode of ancient Greek philosophy (and in everyday speech as well) that we are composed of body and soul. Science, of course, knows of no such thing as "soul". But, as we have already seen, neither did the ancient Jews, at least in the sense that Greeks, or even modern Christians and many others, like the Hindus, do. True, the Hebrew scriptures at times seem to speak of a shadowy existence after death, either pessimistically referring to those who went down to *sheol* (the "pit" or grave) or more optimistically about those who are in "the bosom of Abraham". Still it may surprise us, despite most Christian translations of the Old Testament, to find out that the ancient Hebrews had no such word as "soul" or its equivalent, at least not in the sense that traditional Christian thought has assigned to it.

The Hebrew word *nephesh* is usually translated as "soul", but this is far too narrow of a translation. The word (which actually seems to have been derived from the word meaning "throat") can mean all sorts of things: life, person, self, indeed, any living thing, or sometimes (no doubt reflecting on our most persistent appetite) simply "desire". No doubt such ancient ideas were still quite confused, even to the extent that they seem to have imagined that life somehow resided in the blood. That in turn accounts for a major feature of Jewish dietary laws, the prohibition against eating any meat with blood in it. Still, their idea of life was not so much a thing as an activity, and a rather expansive one at that. Hence another Hebrew word, *kabod*, is also sometimes translated "soul", but literally means "glory", "honor" or even "wealth".

From this it should be evident that from the ancient biblical point of view that it is not some kind of immortal, spiritual substance called "soul" that gives life. Instead, life is a gift and it is God's *ruah* or "wind", "breath", or "spirit" that gives life. When God breathes this spirit into the *bashar* or "flesh", only then does it become a *nephesh*, a living being (Gen. 2:7). Or on the contrary, take away God's *ruah* or "spirit", and living beings simply return to dust (Psalm 104:29).

Certainly, this very much down-to-earth Hebrew picture of human life and death was later modified by inroads of certain Greek, and possibly even Egyptian, ideas concerning a "soul" and the afterlife. Among the deuterocanonical books, the Book of Wisdom (or Wisdom of Solomon) shows definite Greek influences in this respect. Later on, medieval Judaism developed its own cabbalist mysticism that was heavily influenced by

Neo-platonist ideas about the soul, even to the point of seeming to adopt in some cases such non-biblical concepts as the pre-existence of the soul or even theories of reincarnation.

Contemporary Judaism, on the other hand, has tended to hew more closely to the ancient biblical mode of thought, even to the point of generally ignoring the later biblical development of belief in a resurrection—which obviously would play into Christian hands. In this, some strains of Jewish conservatism bear a striking resemblance to modern scientific agnosticism in these matters.

This is not to say that the Hebrew scriptures and contemporary science are entirely in agreement on what makes us alive. Evolutionary science sees life as a "property" of matter—given sufficient complexity under the right conditions, not as a result of some mysterious divine "breath". But the two views agree completely on the basic materiality of human nature. We are rooted in our earthiness. "Man [*Adam*]" was made out of "the dust of the ground [*adamah*]" (Gen. 2:7). Of ourselves we are merely "dust, and to dust we shall return" (Gen. 3:19).

Thus we see again why the Jews of old could only think of life after death, at least any such after-life worth living, as the effect of what came to be called, by New Testament times, "resurrection"—that is, to rise or to be raised up again. This, in turn, was imagined to be more or less literally the result of God breathing his spirit back into the bodies of the dead that they might live anew. And again, as we have seen, there is no reason to think that Jesus himself saw things any differently. As a Jew, he believed, as did most of the Pharisees in the resurrection. This was against the conservative skepticism of the Sadducees. And this resurrection would be apparently not just of the "just" or righteous, but also even of the wicked—otherwise it is hard to explain the "fire and brimstone" nature of the punishments awaiting them.

Nevertheless, it was St. Paul, not Jesus, who has given Christianity the most nuanced and expansive view of resurrection. By adapting the more sophisticated Greek vocabulary, but still basing himself on the same ancient Hebrew view of human nature, where *bashar* (body) plus *ruah* (spirit) equals *nephesh* (a living person), Paul was able to add a new twist or two to the still developing concept of "resurrection". But in doing so he also introduced a problem or two. One of these has to do with his use of the Greek term *psychê*.

For many Greeks, particularly those influenced by platonic ideas, the *psychê* was an eternal, immortal "soul" or immaterial "substance" which, much the same as the Hindu idea of *atman*, keeps coming back through a process of reincarnation into a series of earthly lives in different bodies. Although the basic concept of an immortal "soul" seems to have contributed to the development of some lines of Jewish thought at that time, both mainstream Judaism and Christianity had to nevertheless reject the idea of the soul's eternal preexistence and the idea that we have more than one chance to live our life as being incompatible with biblical revelation. The attempt of one early Christian theologian, Origen, to incorporate such notions into his approach to Christianity, even as modified by a later Neoplatonic mysticism, was to result in his later condemnation.

Today, despite the widespread use of the term "psychology", most contemporary thought has also rejected such ideas. Not only is the concept of a "soul" as existing apart or independently from a body held to be unverifiable in scientific terms, but even the concept of a "soul" as existing apart from its association with, or even its origin in, a specific body makes the idea of "reincarnation" or "transmigration of souls" highly problematic. If you or I have become who we are in terms of our race, or sex, or specific location in time, then to speak of the soul, much less ones "self" returning to life in a different body or as a member of a different race or of the opposite sex becomes a contradiction in terms.

All this leads us, especially given his own Jewish background, to suspect that in his use of the Greek term *psychê* Paul really meant simply the *nephesh*, the living being or person on what we could call the psychological level of human existence. Indeed, in some places Paul substitutes the Greek term *nous* ("mind") where we would expect to find the word *psychê*. Instead, when Paul speaks of immortality, he uses a quite different term, the word *pneuma* or "spirit". But first and foremost in Paul, the "spirit" is God's spirit, the *ruah Yahweh* of Hebrew thought, the same being the "Holy Spirit" or the "Spirit of Jesus" who raised Christ from the dead. On the other hand, for Paul, there is also such a thing as the human "spirit", as well as the "spirit of this world"—so not all "spirits" are divine or even necessarily good.

Yet as soon as we look at the way Paul generally used the word *pneuma* or "spirit" we should notice something else. Even when he speaks of the human being, we will see that our "spirit" is not so much a thing as it is a quality or a capacity that points toward another distinct level of life beyond that of the mere body or psyche/mind. This closely corresponds to one meaning of *nephesh* as a "desire" or "appetite". So too, Paul speaks (see Romans 8:16) about "our spirit" reaching out, as it were, to "God's Spirit". In other words, our lives are limited and incomplete without God. Without God's life-giving spirit our bodies as well as our "minds" or so-called "souls" are doomed to death. Only God's spirit, the "Holy Spirit" or "the

Spirit of Jesus" who raised him from the dead, can guarantee the longing of our spirit for eternal life.

Accordingly, it was very important for Paul to emphasize the *spiritual* quality of the resurrection. Paul's understanding of resurrection was not simply that of human bodies being restored to life, as a more primitive view might imagine—that would be mere "resuscitation". Instead, for Paul, resurrection is a transformation of "natural" life into a whole new realm of existence. In a passage where he compares the first Adam to the second (Christ) we can gain a keen insight into the evolution of Paul's thought about resurrection.

> If there is a natural body, there is a spiritual body too. So the first man, Adam, as scripture says, became a living soul; and the last Adam has become a life-giving spirit. But first came the natural body not the spiritual one; that came only afterwards. The first man, being made of earth, is earthy by nature; the second man is from heaven. The earthly man is the pattern for earthly people, the heavenly man for heavenly ones. And as we have borne the likeness of the earthly man, so shall we bear the likeness of the heavenly one.
>
> (I Corinthians 15:45-49)

If I have used both the words "evolution" and "transformation" to describe what I think I see in the above passage, it is also because we can see a whole new mode of thinking about human nature revealed here. The "living soul" who is represented by Adam (*psychên zôosan* are the Greek words Paul used in this passage instead of simply *psychê*— but here it seems likely that he was thinking of the Hebrew *nephesh*) is succeeded by Christ who has become a "life-giving spirit" (*pneuma zôopoioun*). This is why Paul sometimes calls the Holy Spirit the "Spirit of Jesus", that is, the spirit that transformed the earthly Jesus into the "heavenly" or glorified Lord Christ.

Also, I think we can see in the above passage a change, not just from a more earthly concept of resurrection, from a primitive view of a mere resuscitation of a corpse—the kind of thing for which Paul was ridiculed in his preaching at Athens (Acts 17:32). Here we have a more advanced view, one describing a breakthrough into a new level of existence. It is also a view that, if it is correct, in turn raises the idea of evolutionary progress to a whole new level of understanding.

We are always, or at least should be, in the process of becoming more human. This is not just true of the beginning stages as we develop into fully formed embryos from mere specks of reproductive matter or even after we are born as squalling infants to gradually become children who learn to speak or eventually young people who think on their own. Nor do we suddenly come to our adulthood or "majority" at some arbitrary age, with it all downhill from there. No, we can continue to evolve even in the direction of the spirit—a never finished task, which, if anything, should be accelerated by the onset of mid-life, and old age. In this way, every human life can be said to be an evolution individually in itself.

But there is more to it than that. There is also the whole collective dimension to this evolution. Modern science, at its best—when it isn't devising ever more horrible weapons—has dedicated itself to improving humanity's condition and making this world a better and longer-lasting place. This drive toward human progress should show us that evolution is not just a mechanism that results in ever higher and more complex forms of biological life, but is also an impulse or energy in human nature which impels us to surpass ourselves searching for a better and ever more fulfilling level of existence. Philosophers sometimes speak of this as the human drive or desire for *transcendence*, which literally means to go beyond where or what we are. But transcendence must be more than just a desire to go beyond what we are as mere individuals. It must be also a *self-transcendence* in the sense of transcending or going beyond concern for self.

So too in biblical thought. Redemption or salvation is not just a matter of individual "soul-saving". For St. Paul, the movement towards transcendence was not just a case of individual human longing for salvation but of *all* creation, which as depicted by Paul (see Romans 8:20-21) has been "made subject to frustration" or "vanity". So it is not just the fate of individual humans but also the fate of all creation that concerned Paul. But again, Paul's answer is to be found in the power of God—the power of the Spirit—that power that raised Jesus from the dead, and which will raise us also, so that by finally defeating death in all its forms, Christ can turn over the redeemed universe back to the Father "that God may become all in all" (see I Corinthians 15:28).

What we see here is, I would submit, a greatly expanded view not just of resurrection, but of redemption as well. I think it also may give us the key to a whole new way of understanding the divinity of Jesus Christ.

Jesus in Evolution towards God

We know that the concept of "evolution" involves not just the development or growth of things from birth to death, but also implies the transformation from one level of life to, or into, another. It has been this idea of the "transmutation of species" that has been most controversial, particularly when it has come to the area of human origins. While part of the problem may seem only to be semantic—humankind's "descent" from the ape should be more accurately described as being humanity's "ascent" from a now extinct species of primate—there are nevertheless real puzzles. For example, it is probably easier to explain a degenerative evolution or "devolution" by means of the biological understanding of atrophy (that "what isn't used disappears") than it is to explain how any species acquires new advanced characteristics.

In somewhat the same way, although the earliest New Testament christologies spoke of Jesus being raised to his position as Lord—thus a "low christology" that begins with his humanity and "ascends" to his divinity— it is probably easier to think in terms of divine power which has no limits, and of God "descending" into the human condition. Later New Testament christology, and almost all official Church teaching, has been in this latter "high" christological mode, so much so that most modern attempts to revive the low christology of ascent, if not condemned as outright heretical, have been viewed as "dangerous to the faith".

Nevertheless, at the same time, traditional Christian teaching, with the exception of some lines of Reformation theology, has always held an "ascending" approach when it comes to the doctrine of what is generally called "sanctifying grace". Unlike Protestant (especially Lutheran) theology which held that grace only "justifies" us—that is, covers over our sinfulness to make us acceptable to God—the traditional Catholic doctrine of grace has always held that human life is transformed or elevated to a new level of existence, one that makes our lives and our persons "holy" in a special way. This sanctifying grace was also distinguished from the lesser "actual graces". These latter were seen as divine helps to become better persons in various ways such as acquiring good habits, overcoming temptations, etc. Sanctifying grace, on the other hand, was seen as a sharing in divine life, although in a derivative, creaturely form.

But the Eastern Christian (both Orthodox and Catholic) tradition went even farther, viewing this grace as "uncreated", that is, not just as a share in godlike qualities, but as an actual participation in the divine life— hence the doctrine of *theopoesis* (usually shortened to *theosis*) or the "divinization" or virtual "deification" of the human being through grace. Indeed, it can be said that this theme, as derived from the promise of our being "able to share the divine nature" (see II Peter 1:4) has played a central role in Eastern Christian theology, so much so that it has led to another theological rift, this time between the Eastern and the Western Church, this time over the whole idea of what we mean by "supernatural" in reference to the whole concept of "grace".

On the one hand we have western insistence (and here I mean Protestant as well as Roman Catholic—both deriving from the Augustinian theological tradition) on the use of the word "grace" (*charis*) in a way that emphasizes its sheer gratuity as a gift from God. It was seen as in no way owed to us, with human nature seen as being fixed and naturally complete, consisting of a mortal body and an immortal soul. Thus everything above and beyond what is strictly human is in some way "supernatural". According to this view of human nature, borrowed from or at least re-enforced by Platonist philosophy, the soul survives death because it is "naturally" spiritual. Yet, according to the western Christian theological adaptation of this approach, without "sanctifying grace" this natural immortality or eternity itself might be a dead end. With grace, we get to enjoy heaven and without it, we are consigned to "hell"—or at least to "limbo" in the opinion of those who could not accept Augustine's view of the fate of unbaptized babies who would otherwise be deprived of eternal happiness through no fault of their own

In contrast to this, Eastern Christian theology has always been uneasy with such a rigid division between what is "natural" and what is "supernatural". From one point of view, it sees *all* of creation as a gift. But on the other hand, it sees the true or full, and therefore to some extent "natural", human destiny as being to share in God's life. Hence, to the eastern mentality, to call grace "supernatural", makes it sound like an add-on, like a hat placed on a head, on top of what is already a complete human nature. This is seen as distorting the true situation; where humans, created in God's "image", are called achieve "likeness" to God. Thus, in contrast to the western tendency to reduce the effect of grace to "justification" (as seen especially in Reformation theology), easterners tend to see the effect of divine grace to be primarily a share or participation in divine life, not just in the next life, but also even in our life here and now.

But if this alternative way of thinking about the matter were true, then would it not imply that human nature, taken by itself, is to some extent incomplete? We may very well need God's help or graces to reach heaven, but, it would seem, we also need it to become just even *fully human* as well.

If so, then the real division is not between what is natural and what is supernatural; although theoretically, I suppose such a division does exist. Instead what is of much more significance is the division between what God creates and what is "uncreated"—which is to say, God himself. Grace, then, at least the truly sanctifying kind, is no mere holy "thing" or a commodity of sorts, a mere ticket (but indeed precious ticket) to heaven. It is a participation in the life of the uncreated Creator; hence the life of grace is a "divinized" life. Through it we not only share divine life, but we ourselves even become, as it were, God!

Yet this very traditional doctrine of the "divinization" or "deification" of human beings, even if it sounds somewhat strange to western ears, stands in a rather odd contrast to the way such an approach has been excluded from our more traditional ways of looking at Christ, even in the eastern tradition. I suppose this is due to the belief that because Christ is God, he must always be considered primarily as the "divinizer" rather than the divinized.

True, there was a whole vein of what is today called "Spirit Christology" in early Christian thought, largely associated with the School of Antioch in Syria, that also very much emphasized the humanity of Jesus as revealed in the gospels, particularly in the synoptic gospels. In this line of thought, it is the Holy Spirit that descends upon Jesus at his baptism, leads or drives him into the desert, gives him power over evil spirits, and raised him from the dead (Romans 8:11). This was also, to put it in more contemporary terms, a "low christology" and it was eventually to pass into disfavor under accusations of "adoptionism" and other related heresies, to be replaced by the domination of the "high christology" of the Johannine gospel and of the Alexandrian school.

This is strange in a way, and in view of the doctrine of human divinization, unfortunate. It has tended to set aside Christ in such a way that all the things the gospels say about Jesus as a human can't be easily taken at face value—things like his psychological suffering as well as his physical suffering, his temptations, and certainly not, heaven forbid, his faith!

Yet if we wish to look at the life of Jesus from the viewpoint of his own faith, a "low" christology of "ascent" is an altogether necessary presupposition. For we have already seen that the life of faith is a life lived unrelentingly in a spirit of self-sacrifice in total and complete abandonment to the will of God. Jesus may well have displayed miraculous power, prophetic knowledge, and divine compassion, but none of this was equal to the love he showed when he laid down his life for others through a total act of trust and faith in God. Even the Gospel of John exalts this moment of self-sacrifice as the moment of glory and moment of the triumph of God's all-consuming love.

Of course, the whole problem here, when we look at it this way, is that the call of Christian discipleship, like the promise of "divinization" itself, is seen as putting us all on an equal footing, as it were, with Christ. Being told that we must become like him ("other Christs"), traditional main-stream "high christology" seems to do an about-face, always quick to remind us that of, course, he was "different". No doubt he was, but the question is, just how?

Probing the Difference

If the question of Christ's uniqueness is held to be all-important, the answer is even more important—and problematic.

In contemporary christological debate, it has become commonplace to express concern that our understanding of Jesus, if it is to remain "orthodox", must be such as to establish his difference from the rest of humans in terms of *kind,* rather than simply in terms of *degree.* Thus it is often held that the touchstone of Christian orthodoxy is the confession that Jesus Christ is different in "kind" from the rest of us, in that he alone is, among all humans, at the same time, really, truly God, and this because he always was so in the person of the divine "Word" or "Son". In this way, a so-called "high christology" or "christology of descent" is held to be altogether necessary for a full understanding of the truth, no matter how helpful a low christology may be in helping us understand Jesus from a human point of view.

Put in these terms I'm inclined to agree. Low christologies or christologies of "ascent", like that which I appear to be favoring, are typically faulted for reducing the difference between Christ and us as being simply one of degree. This is taken to imply that his divine identity is being denied or simply reduced to being an example, even if *the* preeminent example, of "divinization".

Yet I'm also greatly in sympathy with theologian Robert MacAffie Brown's warning that to the extent we insist on Christ's *difference* from us in the language of high christology, to that extent we end up denying his true humanity. Too much stress on a supposed difference in kind ends up making him into an altogether different species, a kind of *"E.T."* (an "extra terrestrial"), an alien form of life, sharing some affinity for humanity, but nevertheless distinctly different. In fact, it should not go unnoticed how the film by that name some years back was seen by a few Christian reviewers as a parable of the Incarnation. Is this how we really wish Jesus to be understood?

I really don't think so. If we must choose between seeing him as different in "kind" or simply different in "degree", I think we find ourselves facing an impossible situation, an "either/or" dichotomy, either of which, understood strictly on such terms, amounts to heresy. If "different in kind" is our answer, then we really end up denying his humanity. But on the other hand, if it is simply a difference of "degree", then we end up putting his divinity into doubt.

To try to avoid this dilemma I would call attention to an ancient maxim cited by St. Athanasius in the East and St. Augustine in the West as well as by many other early theologians as far back as St. Irenaeus in the second-century. Again and again we find it repeated, even as late as the thirteenth-century, even by someone as theologically precise as St. Thomas Aquinas, that "God became man so that man might become God".

I think that this saying (updated perhaps in more gender inclusive language—not that it was ever taken in any other way) sums up, in two short phrases, the highest expression of christology and soteriology as well. Of course, it needs to be explained or "unpacked". But, rather than concentrating on the first half, which is the christological problem, let's look again at the second part of the saying, but this time at the metaphysical implications of the assertion that humans can "become God".

Strictly speaking, of course, God alone is (or ever can be) God. Divinity as such is incommunicable. Augustine, who used the maxim in its original form (in *Sermo 27 de Tempore* as quoted above) also qualified it somewhat when on another occasion he paraphrased it to write, "The only Son of God became a son of man to make many men sons of God" (*Sermo 194*). Certainly this qualification is what one might expect from him who has been dubbed "The Doctor of Grace", even though "sons" in the last use of that word in the above quote is obviously meant in the sense of merely adopted children of God.

On the other hand, might we not say (although with less precision) that not just humanity through "grace", but *all* creation is, in a way, "adopted"— not in simply having been created by God, but in the sense of its continued existence being dependent on God, that is, by "divine concurrence". Yet if we go back to considering why anything exists in the first place (the basic philosophical question as to why there is anything rather than nothing) we are brought back to the fundamental concept of God as "Being" (Augustine) whose primary quality or attribute is, as some of the medieval philosophers put it "*aseitas*", that is, being or existence in and of itself. Thus God's most basic "property" is to *exist*, indeed, to be God is to be in such a way that all other existence is, in itself, a *participation* in God's being, or to put it in still another way, made more popular in recent times by theologian Paul Tillich God is the "Ground of Being".

Tillich's terminology, however, is hardly new. It seems to have been borrowed from the fourteenth-century German mystical theologian Johann Eckhart—who in his sermons spoke of God as "Ground". Eckhart also went so far as to proclaim that in itself to exist is to be God, at least in the sense that everything that is, insofar as it exists, partakes in the divine quality of existence as such and therefore to exist is, at least in some sense, to already be divine!

But normally we don't speak this way (especially after Eckhart was hauled before the Inquisition and accused of pantheism), because you and I have only a borrowed existence. No matter how holy or complete we become, our existence as individuals is but a derived existence. Even when raised by "grace" or the Holy Spirit to participate in God's life, we at best are "divine" as adopted sons or daughters of God. To suggest that existing as isolated individuals we can somehow actually be or become God or to be ontologically "the Son of God"—as the critics misunderstood Eckhart to be saying—is of course metaphysically impossible or absurd. Only God can be God as such.

However, it is less commonly pointed out that strictly speaking, the first part of the statement that "God became man" is just as impossible. Only a "man" (a human being with all its limitations) can be truly human. Ontologically speaking (which is to say, in the order of being), God as such cannot actually be a human or become one. That would seem to be a metaphysical contradiction in terms.

Nevertheless, human life, insofar as we exist, shares God's existence. So too, looked at from the divine perspective—if we can presume to do so—God's creating and sustaining role in the universe (divine "concurrence") implies that no event in nature, or in our activities, or any imaginable activity of any sort in the universe is accomplished without God's presence. So in this sense of divine *immanence*, all that exists is divine. This is just the flip side of Eckhart's "existence is God" rightly understood.

Taking such ontological restrictions seriously, then it would seem that strictly speaking to say "God became man" is just as impossible as to say "Man can become God". From this point of view, a christology of "descent" seems to be as impossible as one of "ascent". Nevertheless, in the order of divine concurrence it is possible to say that God "descends" into humanity, just as surely, and perhaps with much greater certainty than we can say any particular human "ascends" to divinity or participation in God's life.

The reason for this is because God is the altogether necessary precondition or ground of existence. Our existence is entirely contingent on God's existence, even if our individual identity, rooted in our physicality, marks each of us as distinct from our creator. But in the case of Jesus, was not only his existence, much as ours, entirely contingent on God, but even more, was not his individual identity as a human in some very unique way identified personally with God's concurrence in human history? If so, then I think we come as close as we can to saying that God has incarnated himself in a human life as it is possible to do. Yet this would be without destroying what it means to be a human being, or, on the other hand, without the primary agent of that concurrence ceasing to be God. In this way we might say that not only the degree of divine in every aspect of the life of the man Jesus, but even more the clarity with which this has been revealed, is how he may have been preeminently different than us.

Would even this make him different in "kind"? Perhaps not really, when you get down to it. Yet I would see another aspect, a temporal one, as well, that does add to his preeminence. From this temporal aspect, the difference between Jesus and us, I would submit, is that from the very beginning, that is, from the first moment of his actual existence as a human, the fullness of the Holy Spirit was there. Not only that, but even before his conception, from all eternity—if we can speak of a "before" in respect to eternity—that this fullness of the divine spirit was intended by God. In this sense Jesus was absolutely "predestined" as the summit of all divinized humanity. There never was, nor, as far as we know, will there ever be a union between God and man as complete as his.

This is not to say that he was necessarily conscious of this fact as a human. Instead he appears to have slowly—or perhaps more quickly at some times than others—grown into full consciousness of this union between himself and God. It may even be that the summit of this consciousness was not reached until after his death and that his resurrection was the outward sign of this totally conscious consummation.

Furthermore, I could add a certain ontological slant to this divine immanence and indwelling as well. If we can say that God exists in or "subsists" (which is to say supports or gives existence to) the person whom we call Jesus—which is true of all persons—still in the case of Jesus would it not be possible to say that the indwelling of God was so intense that he was already raised to a higher level of existence?

Here I'm thinking of Engel's evolutionary principle that enough difference or increase in *quantity* can amount to a difference in *quality* as well. For example, few would doubt that humans are qualitively different from mere animals, yet when we try to account for that difference, we seem, at least according to evolutionary evidence, to be reduced to concluding that the greatly increased quantity or amount of thinking ability is what makes this difference possible. As Teilhard de Chardin was wont to say: "Animals know, but man knows that he knows."

In a parallel fashion, might it not be then that in the case of Jesus, the absolute influx of divine grace at the beginning of his existence as a human being made a *qualitative* difference in the meaning of the second part of the saying "... that man might become God"? If a person's thinking and willing become, due to the influx of divine grace, totally one with that of God, can it not be said that person has become fully one with God, at least to the extent that any creature could be said to become "divinized" in this way?

Finally, if such considerations still seem to smack too much of a "low" christology, no matter how high the ascent, I would suggest that we consider the divine initiative or influx of grace into Jesus in an even more radical and personalizing way. If, as we have seen, no human person is complete or fully human without the influx of the Holy Spirit, could we not say that so complete was this divine influx into the composition of Jesus' humanity, that his personhood was that of God's archetypical plan for all humans? If so, it would to be to say that this archetype (the true "Adam") has taken shape fully in this man, and because this archetype is, at the same time, God's expression or "Word" about himself. "Let us make man in our own image ... in the image of God he created him " (Gen. 1:26,27). Thus Christ is also the perfect "image of the invisible God" (Col. 1:15).

If so, then it seems that the only real barrier, even within a high christology, towards seeing Jesus as fully human, as well as fully divine, is the false dichotomy that is set up when we presuppose that on the one hand, that human beings are complete, fully conscious, fully self-sufficient creatures all by themselves, and, on the other hand, that the divine "Word" or "Son" whom we presuppose Jesus to have been (in his divine nature) was himself a complete, fully-conscious "person" in his own right apart from the existence of Jesus in his humanity. That this last observation (first suggested by Dutch theologian Piet Schoonenburg in his book *The Christ*, as far as I know) seems to undercut the traditional understanding of the Trinity, may be true, but then it also brings me to what I feel, at least for now, must be my concluding remarks.

A "Monotheocentric" Faith

By way of a theological summary to this whole book I would have to say this: if it is to remain faithful to its origins, Christian belief, which includes our faith in Christ, must be at most a universalized version of Jesus' own faith. Anything else must be viewed as a deviation from that norm.

Such a faith is, above all, a belief in *one* God, in other words, an uncompromising *monotheism*. All trinitarian elaborations, whatever be their beauty or profundity, must be held subservient to that central tenet. The God of Jesus, his "Father" and ours, is the God revealed to Israel. And that God is one!

Furthermore, we must always keep in mind the basic revelatory function of Christ. Even if we believe him to be divine, it is obvious from the New Testament that the mission of Jesus was not to make himself worshipped, but to direct all attention to the Father. Believing what we do about him, we Christians may be forgiven our enthusiasm and proclivity to make Jesus Christ our central cult figure, but this is not following most faithfully in the footsteps of Jesus himself. In other words, "Christianity", despite its name, must always be *theocentric*, not "christocentric" at heart.

Keeping these two central points in mind, even when we enter the realm of trinitarian elaboration, we must always keep it subservient to the *kerygmatic* demands of the New Testament—the liberating Gospel or "good news." We must always remember, historically speaking, that the Christian doctrine of the Trinity emerged out of the prior necessity of explaining how Jesus Christ, through the power of God's Spirit, is the revelation of the one God whom Jesus addressed as "Father". In more technical terms, "immanential" trinitarianism, which is speculation upon the *inner* workings of the divine nature, must remain secondary to and dependent on "economic" trinitarianism, which is to say, upon the work of God in relation to salvation history. Otherwise, Christian thought opens itself up to the charge of theological—or dare I say "mystical"?— adventurism.

Nor is this trinitarian trend even uniquely Christian. Plato seems to have developed a trinitarian view of divine nature, one that may even have it roots in Vedic or Hindu thought. And if one were to read the Roman philosopher Plotinus (205-270 AD) one cannot help wondering just how much his mystical reworking of Plato influenced Christian doctrine as it took shape in those early years. So too, some more recent western philosophers, such as Hegel and Whitehead, devised their own trinitarian insights. Christians may well rejoice at all this, or even see it as a providential working of God's grace, but we would do well to take all claims of insight into the inner nature of God with a grain of salt.

In addition, even within the realm of an "economic" trinitarianism that claims to adhere strictly to the New Testament, we must also remember that even such scriptural Johannine and Pauline themes as the pre-existence of the divine Word/Wisdom/Son are "third level" traditions. As explained in the very beginning of this book, most of these must be understood as inspired theological elaborations. Otherwise we run into great difficulty in explaining what appear to be evident contradictions. Even the personalization of the Spirit in John's gospel would not seem to meet the strict criteria of having been part of the remembered words or deeds of the historical Jesus. Otherwise how explain the complete absence of this approach in the rest of the New Testament? Nor do these themes appear to be part of the original *kerygma* as well. For this reason, none of them should be taken as the only possible approach. The same should be said about the various soteriological themes in the New Testament, whether expressed in terms of "justification", "enlightenment", or "cosmic restoration". They could be seen more as complementary than definitive.

So too must something similar be said about what we might term "the fourth level" of tradition—the creeds and other post-scriptural theological elaborations formulated early in the history of Christian thought. Such formulations as "one nature, three persons" to summarize the Trinity, or "one person, two natures" to describe Christ, are all too subject to misunderstanding. Indeed, perhaps the most respected Catholic theologian of the twentieth-century, Karl Rahner, suggested a moratorium the term "person" in the trinitarian context, the contemporary usage of the term being too far from what the ancient Church theologians were trying to convey.

Finally, and most of all, the same must be said about contemporary attempts (including this one) to make sense of everything. While I have found myself increasingly resistant to the ancient Christian practice of extolling paradox as a sign of God's working in this world, which seems to me to be deliberate "mystification", still, I have to admit that there is more than enough mystery in it to keep theologians occupied until the end of time. So maybe the important thing is not so much to slavishly hew to theological correctness, trying to explain or fully understand all that has been believed about Jesus. Instead, I believe that it is much more important to be a Christian—to walk simply and humbly in the footsteps of Jesus, "the leader and perfecter of faith."

My reason for emphasizing this should be obvious by now. Religious divisiveness remains one of the greatest, if not the only, cause of human conflict upon this earth. Religion, which should be the greatest unifier of humanity—"May they all be one…as you are in me and I am in you" (John 17:21)—has become, sadly to say, almost from the very beginning, a point of contention. Perhaps this is to be expected in view of religion's role in providing what for most people is the ultimate meaning of their life in this world, even if their religious beliefs focus largely on whatever is next. The advent of Christianity, unfortunately, did not alleviate this situation. If anything, it seems to have only made it worse. One cause—not the only one, but certainly one that is a major premise of this book—is that *faith*, which is a measure of our fundamental trust in God, has been too often and for too long confused with *belief* or beliefs, which to a large extent are views, opinions, or attempts to formulate exactly why we may have such trust or confidence. Except for his conviction that the reign of God in some way already was among us or was soon to be fulfilled, Jesus was noteworthy in having introduced no new beliefs beyond those—including the resurrection of the dead—already held by many, perhaps most, of his fellow Jews. All that he asked for was a life lived in trustful faith in God and a faithful love of God and ones fellow human beings. If Christianity introduced any new doctrines, they have originated more from his followers, not from Jesus himself.

If this last chapter or extended "christological" postscript may have seemed to concentrate on the latter (the conflicting beliefs regarding the divine-human identity of Jesus and my attempt to present a possible solution to the problem), it is only for the sake of accentuating the former, that is, his role as a model for our faith. And if this view of Jesus—as a man of faith—seems as unorthodox to some as my views concerning his ultimate identity, then I must conclude, more than ever, that beliefs (including my own, however tentative they may be) continue to be an obstacle rather than an asset to authentic faith.

Appendix

On the Translation of Hebrews 12:1b-2a

The passage from the Epistle to the Hebrews with which I attempted to set the whole tone of this book (see the *Foreword*) is the only place in the New Testament where the faith of Jesus is, I believe, directly spoken of. But it is also one of the most controversial passages of the Bible, particularly when it comes to any agreement in translation. A comparative look at the various renditions might give the reader some inkling of the difficulty, but perhaps even Just a glimpse of the core section of this passage in its original Greek (even in transliterated Greek with a literal translation of each word beneath) will give the reader at least a vague idea of what the translators are working with.

di	*hupomonês*	*trechômen*	*ton*	*prokeimenon*	*hêmin*	*agôna*
through	endurance	let us run	the	set before	us	contest
aphorôntes	*eis*	*ton*	*tês*	*pisteôs*	*archêgon*	*kai*	*teleiôtên*
looking away	to	the	of the	faith	author (?)	and	finisher (?)
Iêsoun...						
Jesus						

The nub of the conflict has been the correct meaning of the word *archêgon* and to a lesser extent, of the word *teleiôtên*. The vast majority of English translations, including various Protestant and even the latest *New Revised Standard Version* and *New International Version* translations, continue to follow or be strongly influenced by St. Jerome's rendering of the Greek word *archêgon* with the Latin *auctor* or "author" while the older version of the *Catholic New American Bible* translated the word with the verb "inspires". *The Jerusalem Bible* and *New Jerusalem Bible* both transpose this noun as well as the correlative term *teleiôtên* into a participles, thus speaking of Jesus as "leading us" in our faith, and bringing this faith to "perfection".

But the translations using "author" or similar terms avoiding the word "leader" are ignoring the normal accepted biblical usage of the word *archêgon*. True, the word can mean "author", but this was in early Homeric or classical "Attic" Greek, not later biblical Greek. The "*koine*" or common marketplace Greek of the New Testament is closer to the Greek of the Septuagint translation of the Hebrew (Old Testament) scriptures in which the word *archêgon* means "prince" (the one who is first) or "leader" (see Arndt & Gingrich, *A Greek-English Lexicon of the New Testament and Other Early Christian Literature*, University of Chicago Press, 1957). Nor does the word *teleiôtên* really mean "perfector" except in a derivative sense. Literally it means "to reach a goal" (*telos*) or to "reach an end", or to "finish" or as in the context of this image, to "complete" a race.

No doubt the usual translation of the words in chapter 12 has also been influenced by the same combination of words found earlier in 2:10 of the same epistle, where it is said that Jesus was "made perfect" (*teleiôsai*) through suffering as *archêgon* of their salvation (*tês sôtêrias autôn*). This becomes even more evident where the *tês pisteos* in chapter 12:2a is translated "of our faith" where the plural possessive pronoun *autôn* does not appear in the original Greek text translated by St. Jerome. Instead the word *tês* is simply the usual Greek definite article, which at most would give us "of the faith", but which, in the peculiar style of Greek grammar where the genitive case of the article is not to be translated at all, the normal meaning would simply be "of faith".

Hence we can see two general trends of translation pitted against each other here. It is clear that the author of the Epistle to the Hebrews, who otherwise was not at all reticent about upholding the divinity of Christ, nevertheless, unlike his translators, conveys a meaning that holds up Jesus as a model or example of faith and (as in 6:19) our "forerunner" (*prodromos*) in hope. Thus it is not just a faith that consists in "trust" but conveys a sense of dogged *perseverance* or *commitment* that has its basis on definite convictions—"for the sake of the joy..." The most accurate modern translations attempt to convey this same dynamic notion of faith.

All this is in contrast to the general run of older translations which, apparently fearing that the literal sense of the words might confuse the faithful, substitute a reading that emphasizes Jesus as the origin of, or possibly as the object of "our faith" or "the faith". This objectified faith, in turn, would be understood primarily as an adherence to a set of beliefs rather than the gospel sense of a venturing forth in a loving trust in God.

Bibliography

NOTE: The following list of titles, both old and new, is a list of works dealing with the life of Jesus and the subject of christology and other related topics which have influenced the author's thought over the past forty years. It does not pretend to be a compilation of all of the books available on the subject.

Adam, Karl. *The Christ of Faith; The Christology of the Church.* Translated from the German by Joyce Crick, New York; Pantheon. 1957.

_____ *Christ Our Brother.* Translated by Dom Justin McCann, O.S.B. New York. Collier Books, 1962.

Aulen, Gustaf. *Christus Victor: An Historical Study of the Three Main Types of the Idea of the Atonement.* Translated from the Swedish by A. G. Herbert, M.A. New York, Macmillan, 1969.

Badia, Leonard F. *Jesus: Introducing His Life and Teaching.* New York/Mahwah, N.J., Paulist Press, 1985.

Brown, Raymond E. *The Birth of the Messiah: A commentary on the Infancy Narratives in Matthew and Luke.* Garden City, N.Y., Doubleday, 1977.

_____ *The Community of the Beloved Disciple: The Life, Loves, and Hates of an Individual Church in New Testament Times.* New York/Mahwah, N.J., Paulist Press, 1979.

_____ and Meier, John P. *Antioch and Rome.* Ramsey, N.J., Paulist Press, 1983.

Carmody, James M. and Clarke, Thomas E. (Eds.) *Christ and His Mission: Christology and Soteriology.* Westminster, Md., The Newman Press, 1966. (Vol. III in *Sources of Christian Theology.* Ed. By Paul F. Palmer, S.J.)

Cassidy, Richard J. *Jesus, Politics, and Society.* Maryknoll, N.Y.; Orbis Books, 1978.

Cobb, John B., Jr. *Christ in a Pluralistic Age.* Philadelphia, The Westminster Press, 1975.

Congar, Ives M-J, *Christ, Our Lady and the Church.* Translated by Henry St..John, O.P., Westminster, Md., Newman Press, 1957.

Cook, Michael L. *The Jesus of Faith.* New York, Ramsey, and
    Toronto, Paulist Press, 1981.

Crossan, John Dominic. *The Histroical Jesus: The Life of a Medi-*
    terranean Jewish Peasant. New York: Harper Collins, 1993.

Daniel-Rops, Henrí. *Jesus and His Times.* Translated by Ruby Millar.
    Garden City, N.Y., Doubleday, 1958.

Duling, Dennis C. *Jesus Christ Through History.* New York,
    Harcourt Brace Jovanovich, 1979.

Dulles, Avery. *Apologetics and the Biblical Christ.*
    Westminster, Md., Newman Press, 1964.

Durwell, F. X. *The Resurrection: A Biblical Study.* Translated by
    Rosemary Sheed. New York, Sheed and Ward, 1960.

Dupuis, Jacques, S.J. *Christianity and the Religions: From*
    Confrontation to Dialogue. Maryknoll, N.Y.; Orbis, 2002.

Dwyer, John C. *Son of Man and Son of God: A New Language for*
    Faith. New York/Ramsey, N.J., Paulist Press, 1983.

Endo, Shusaku. *A Life of Jesus.* Translated from the Japanese.
    Mahwah, N.J.; Paulist Press, 1978.

Fitzmyer, Joseph A. *A Christological Catechism: New Testament*
    Answers. New York/Ramsey, Paulist Press, 1982.

_____ *Scripture and Christology: A Statement of the Biblical*
    Comission with a Commentary. New York/Mahwah,
    Paulist Press, 1986.

Goergen, Donald J. *The Mission and Ministry of Jesus.*
    Wlimington, Del., Micharel Glazier, 1986.

Griffin, David R. *A Process Christology.* Philadelphia, The
    Westminster Press, 1973.

Grillmeier, Aloys. *Christ in the Christian Tradition.* Vol I,
    translated by John Bowden. Vol II, translated by Pauline
    Allen and John Cawte. Atlanta, John Knox Press, 1965,
    1987.

Guillet, Jacques. *The Consciousness of Jesus.* Translated by Edmond
    Bonin. New York, Newman Press, 1972.

Guitton, Jean. *The Problem of Jesus.* Translated by A. Gordon Smith.
    New York, P.J. Kennedy & Sons, 1972.

_____ *Jesus: The Eternal Dilemma.* Translated by Donald M.
    Antoine. Staten Island, N.Y., Alba House, 1967.

Hart, Thomas N. *To Know and Follow Jesus:Contemporary*
    Christology. New York/Ramsey, Paulist Press,1984.

Harvey, Anthony Ernest. *Jesus and the Constraints of History.* Philadelphia, Westminster Press, 1982.

Haight, Roger. *Jesus the Symbol of God.* Maryknoll, N.Y., Orbis Books, 1999.

Helwig, Monica K. *Jesus, The Compassion of God: New Perspectives on the Tradition of Christianity.* Wilmington, Del., Michael Glazier, 1983.

Jeramias, Joachim. *The Parables of Jesus.* Translated by S.H. Hooke. London, SCM/New York, Charles Scribner's Sons, 1963.

Kasper, Walter. *Jesus The Christ.* Translated by V. Green. London, Burns & Oates/New York, Paulist Press, 1977.

Kee, Howard Clark. *Jesus in History; An Approach to the Study of the Gospels.* New York, Harcourt Brace Jovanovich. 1970, 1977.

Küng, Hans. *On Being A Christian.* Translated by Edward Quinn. Garden City, N.Y., Doubleday, & Co.,1976.

_____ *Eternal Life? Death as a Medical, Philosophical and Theological Problem.* Translated by Edward Quinn. Garden City, N.J.: Doubleday, 1984.

_____ van Ess, Josef; von Stristencron, Heinrich; Bechert, Heinz. *Christianity and the World Religions: Paths of Dialogue with Islam, Hinduism and Buddhism.* Translated by Peter Heinegg. Garden Citry, N.Y. Doubleday & Co., 1985.

Lane, Dermot A. *The Reakity of Jesus: An Essay in Christology.* Dublin: Veritas Publications; New York/Ramsey, N.J., Paulist Press, 1 1975.

Lee, Bernard J., S.M. *The Galilean Jewishness of Jesus:Retrieving the Jewish Origins of Christianity.* New York/Mahwah, N.J., Paulist Press, 1988.

Mackey, James P. *Jesus, the Man and the Myth: A Contemporary Christology.* New York/Ramsey, N.J., Paulist Press, 1979.

Macquarrie, John. *Jesus Christ in Modern Thought.* Dublin, Trinity Press International, 1990.

Maloney, George A., S.J. *The Cosmic Christ: From Paul to Teilhard.* New York, Sheed & Ward, 1968.

Mauriac, François. *The Life of Jesus.* Translated by Julie Kernan. New York, David McKay Co. 1937.

Meier, John P. *A Marginal Jew: Rethinking the Historical Jesus.* Vols. I, II, III. Garden City, N.Y.; Doubleday, 1991, 1994, 2001.

Moltmann, Jürgen. *The Crucified God: The Cross of Christ as the Foundation and Criticism of Christian Theology.* Translated by James W. Leitch. New York; Harper & Row, 1967.

Neyrey, Jerome H., S.J. *Christ is Community: The Christologies of the New Testament.* Wilmington, Del.; Michael Galazier, 1985.

North, Robert, S.J. *In Search of the Human Jesus.* New York, Cleveland; Corpus Books, 1970.

O'Collins, Gerald. *Interpreting Jesus.* London: Geoffrey Chapman, 1983: Ramsey, N.J., Paulist Press, 1985.

Pannenberg, Wolfhart. *Jesus—God and Man.* Translated by Lewis L. Wilkins and Duane A. Priebe. Philadelphia: Westminster, Press, 1968

Pawlikowski, John T., O.S.M. *Christ in the Light of the Jewish-Christian Dialogue.* New York/Mahwah, N.J., Paulist Press, 1982

Perrin, Norman, *The New Testament: An introduction: Proclamation and Parenesis, Myth and History.* New York, Harcourt Brace Jovanovich, 1974.

_____ *Rediscovering the Teaching of Jesus.* New York: Harper & Row, 1976

Prat. Ferdinand, S.J., *Jesus Christ: His Life,* his *Teachinq and His Work.* Translated by John J. Heenan, S.J. *Mil*iwaukee: Bruce Publishing Co., 1950.

Rahner, Karl, S.J. *Foundations of Christian Faith: An Introduction to the Idea of Christianity.* Translated by William V. Dych. New York: Seabury/Crossroad, 1978.

_____ and Thüsing, Wilhelm. A New Christology. Translated by David Smith and Verdant Green. New York: Seabury/Crossroad, 1980.

Richard, Lucien, O.M.I., What *Are They* Saying About *Christ and World Religions?* New York/Ramsev, N.J.: Paulist Press, 1981.

Robinson, J. A. T. "A New Look at the Fourth Gospel." Lecture delivered at Oxford University, 1976.

Robinson, James M. *A New Quest of the Historical Jesus.* London: SCM Press Ltd., 1959.

Rubenstein, Richard E. *When Jesus Became God: The Epic Fight over Christ's Divinity in the Last Days of Rome.* New York: Harcourt Brace, 1999.

Schillebeeckx, Edward, *Jesus: An Experiment in Christology* Translated by Hubert Hoskins. New York: Seabury, Crossroad, 1979.

_____ *Christ: The Experience of Jesus as Lord.* Translated by John Bowden. New York: Seabury/Crossroad, 1980.

Schoonenberg, Piet, S.J. *The Christ: A God for Man.* London, 1970

Schweitzer, Albert. *The Quest ot the Historzcal Jesus.* Translated by W. Montgomery, B.D. New York: Macmillan, 1961, 1968.

Smulders, Piet, S.J. *The Fathers on Christology: The Development of Christological Dogma from the Bible to the Great Councils.* Translated by Lucien Roy, S.J. De Pere, Wisc.:St. Norbert Abbey Press, 1968.

Sobrino, Jon, S.J. *Christology at the Crossroads.* Translated by John Drury. Maryknoll, N.Y.: Orbis Press, 1978.

Thompson, William N. *The Jesus Debate: A Survey and Synthesis.* New York/Mahwah, N.J.: Paulist Press, 1985.

Vawter, Bruce. *This Man Jesus: An Essay toward a New Testament Christology.* Garden City, N.Y.: Doubleday. 1975.

Books relating to faith development theory:

Babin, Pierre. *Crisis of Faith: The Religious Psychology of Adolescence.* Translated by Eva Fleischner. New York: Herder & Herder, 1963.

Fowler, James W. *Stages of Faith: The Psychology of Human Development and the Quest for Meanina.* New York: Harper & Row, 1981.

_____ *Becoming Adult, Becoming Christian: Adult Development and Christian Faith.* New York: Harper & Row, 1984

Frankl, Viktor E. *Man's Search for Meaning: An Introduction to Logotherapy.* New York: Pocket Books, 1959, 1963.

_____ *The Will to Meaning: Foundations and Applications of Logotherapy.* New York: New American Library, 1969.

_____ *The Unconscious God: Psychotherapy and Theology.* New York: Simon & Schuster, 1975.

Fromm, Eric. *You Shall Be As Gods.* New York: Harcourt Brace & World, 1966.

Gallup, George. *Faith Development in the Adult Life Cycle.* Princeton, N.J.: The Gallup Organization, 1985.

Gorman, Margaret (ed.) *Psychology and Religion: A Reader.* New York/Mahwah, N.J.: Paulist Press, 1985.

Helminiak, Daniel A. *Spiritual Development: An Interdisciplinary Study.* Chicago: Loyola University Press, 1987.

Kropf, Richard W. *Faith: Security & Risk: The Dynamics of Spiritual Growth.* Mahwah, N.J.: Paulist Press, 1990; Eugene, OR: Wipf & Stock Publishers, 2003.

Leean, Constance. *Faith Development in the Adult Life Cycle.* Copyright: The Religious Education Association of United States and Canada, 1985.

Liebert, Elizabeth. *Changing Life Pattern: Adult Development in Spiritual Direction.* Chalice Press, 2000.

Loevinger, Jane. *Ego Development.* San Francisco: Jossey-Bass Publishers, 1977.

Maslow, Abraham H. *Religions, Values, and Peak-Experiences.* New York: Viking Books, 1970.

Merton, Thomas. *The Ascent to Truth.* New York: Harcourt Brace & Co. 1951.

_____ *The Asian Journal of Thomas Merton.* Edited by Naomi Burton, Br. Patrick Hart & James Laughlin. New York: New Directions, 1973.

Smith, Wilfred Cantwell. *Faith and Belief.* Princeton, N.J.: Princeton University Press, 1979.

Tillich, Paul. *The Dynamics of Faith.* New York: Harper & Row, 1957.

Scriptural Reference Books and Other Books Utilized in this Study.

Aland, Kurt (ed.) *Synopsis of the Four Gospels.* United Bible Societies, 1985.

Arndt, William F. & Gingrich, F. Wilbur. *A Greek-English Lexicon of the New Testament and Other Early Christian Literature.* Chicago: Chicago University Press; Cambridge at the University Press, 1957.

Brown, Raymond E., Fitzmyer, Joseph A. & Murphy, Roland E., (eds.). *The Jerome Biblical Commentary.* Engelwood Cliffs, N.J.: Prentice Hall, 1968.

Darton, Michael, (ed.). *A Modern Concordance to the New Testament.* Garden City, N.Y.: Doubleday, 1976.

Funk, Robert W., Hoovers, Roy W. and the Jesus Seminar. *The Five Gospels: The Search for the Authentic Words of Jesus.* New York: Macmillan, 1993.

Hartdegen, Stephen J., O.F.M. *A Chronological Harmony of the Gospels.* Paterson, N.J.: St. Anthony Guild Press, 1945.

Kohlenburger, John R. III. *The NIV Interlinear Hebrew-English Old Testament.* Grand Rapids, MI: Zondervan Publishing House, 1987

Marshall, Alfred (ed. & transl.). *NASB-NIV Parallel New Testament in Greek and English.* Grand Rapids, MI: Zondervan, 1986.

Merk, Augustus, S.J. *Novum Testamentum Graece et Latine.* Rome: Sumptibus Pontifici Instituti Biblici, 1948.

Robinson, James M. (ed.) *The Nag Hammadi Library in English* San Francisco: Harper & Row, 1988..

Senior, Donald (ed.) *The Catholic Study Bible.* New York, Oxford: Oxford University Press, 1990.

Wansbrough. Henry (ed.) *The New Jerusalem Bible.* Garden City, N.Y.: Doubleday & Co., 1985.

Whitaker, Richard E. and Goehring, James E. *The Eerdmans Analytical Concordance to the Revised Standard Version of the Bible.* Grand Rapids, MI: William B. Eerdmans Publishing Co. 1988.

Acknowledgments

Special thanks are due to Mary Flinn and Chris Knight for their help in the final preparation of this manuscript and to Jim Tedrick of Wipf and Stock Publishers for his patient assistance in seeing to its publication.

Most biblical quotations in English are from *The Jerusalem Bible* and *The New Jerusalem Bible* translations, both published in the United States by Doubleday and Company, Inc., Garden City, New York, in 1966 and 1975. The translated quotation from Pierre Emmanuel is from *The Asian Journal of Thomas Merton*, (New York: New Directions, 1973; © Merton Legacy Trust and New Directions Publishers). Other quotations, when employed, have been taken from the works listed in the *Bibliography*.

***

Note on Typography, Punctuation, and Transliterations

This book has been composed by means of Microsoft Word utilizing the 11-point Times New Roman typeface for the body of the text, and subsequently reset for publication with Adobe Acrobat Distiller.

For the sake of more accuracy, punctuation within quotation marks is according to the rule set by Oxford University Press: only that which is contained in the original is to be included within the quotation marks.

In the transliteration of a few Greek words, the letters *eta* and *omega* are signified, respectively, by the accented letters *ê* and *ô*. The letter *h* has been employed to indicate the correct pronunciation of the initial Greek vowels *o* and *u* in certain words. In the transliteration from Hebrew, *sh* is used to render the consonant *shin*.

Due to the limitations of automatic indexing and line spacing shifts that are endemic to many word-processing programs, page references in the index may occasionally be off by a page. The reader's tolerance and forgiveness is appreciated.

Index

www.ingramcontent.com/pod-product-compliance
Lightning Source LLC
Chambersburg PA
CBHW071916160426

42812CB00098B/1132